Patient Participation: the literature

Sally Brearley

BSc(Hons), RGN, Grad DP, MCSP, AKC

Submitted towards the degree of
BSc(Hons) in Nursing Studies from
King's College London

ROYAL COLLEGE OF NURSING
RESEARCH SERIES

Scutari Press

Aims of the Series

To encourage the appreciation and dissemination of nursing research by making relevant studies of high quality available to the profession at reasonable cost.

The RCN is happy to publish this series of research reports. The projects were chosen by the individual research worker and the findings are those of the researcher and relate to the particular subject in the situation in which it was studied. The RCN in accordance with its policy of promoting research awareness among members of the profession commends this series for study but views expressed do not necessarily reflect RCN policy.

Scutari Press

Viking House, 17–19 Peterborough Road,
Harrow, Middlesex HA1 2AX, England

A subsidiary of Scutari Projects, the publishing company of the Royal College of Nursing

© Scutari Press 1990

First published 1990

British Library Cataloguing in Publication Data:

Brearley, Sally
    Patient participation: the literature. – (Royal College
of Nursing research series)
    1. Medical care. Participation of patients
    I. Title   II. Series
    362.1

    ISBN 1-871364-24-8

Typeset by Action Typesetting Ltd., Gloucester
Printed and bound in Great Britain by Billing & Sons, Worcester

Contents

Acknowledgements

I would like to offer many thanks to Professor Jenifer Wilson-Barnett for her help, initially in selecting a subject for review, and then for guidance en route. The final product may not be quite what either of us envisaged; for this I am entirely responsible.

Thanks also to my husband, Peter, for his support throughout – technical, moral and financial!

Sally Brearley

Abstract

The development of the concept of patient participation can be explored from social, historical, psychological and ethical perspectives. Recent initiatives by government and health service management, professionals and consumers illustrate the importance attached to the concept in practice, at the macro-level. Themes from the medical and nursing literature reflect both progressive and reactionary responses to the demand for patient partnership in care.

For the individual patient and his or her family, participation in care can be considered as a continuum from complete activity to complete passivity. The level of participation appropriate depends on the type of health problem experienced and on other, less well-defined, factors. Preparing patients for effective participation involves the professional in providing information and possibly in training patients to elicit information from others.

A review of research related to the active patient model highlights some areas where evidence is sufficient to form a basis for clinical practice, and others worthy of more detailed review. However, an overview suggests that claims made for this approach to patienthood are supported by fragmentary and sometimes inconclusive evidence, based on poorly developed theory. A closer look at nursing research on chronic illness is perhaps more encouraging, indicating a willingness to formulate theory, develop research tools and methods, and meet the challenge of participation in an holistic and family-centred way.

Implications for practice and suggestions for further research are discussed, and, as a foundation for progress, the review concludes by re-examining aspects of the ideology of patient participation.

1 Introduction

THE PURPOSE AND SCOPE OF THIS REVIEW

Patient participation has become a familiar concept; nurses are often urged to involve patients and their families in every stage of care (e.g. McCarthy, 1985). This observation gives rise to a series of questions. For instance:

- What is meant by patient participation?
- How did the concept of patient participation arise, and how has it evolved since?
- What forms can participation take?
- What benefits are thought to accrue to patients and providers from involvement in health care? For instance, is greater involvement linked to better health outcomes?
- How may patient involvement in care be extended and improved?

These are the issues that this review examines.

Chapter 1 introduces the subject and examines theoretical and descriptive literature forming the background for research in the field of patient participation.

Chapters 2 and 3 review research in two areas:

1. studies that attempt to identify and isolate aspects of patient participation and to examine their effects;
2. studies involving a class of patients who, theoretically, have much to gain from increased participation in care (those with chronic health problems).

A more detailed rationale for this approach is presented later, but, in essence, I wish to assess to what extent, and in what forms, the

1

ideology and theory of patient participation is reflected in research.

Chapter 4 discusses the research findings, considers the implications for practice and offers suggestions for further research.

Utilising insights gained from the research literature, chapter 5 briefly re-examines the concept of patient participation in the light of recent criticisms levelled against it. This re-evaluation is necessary if developments in research and practice are to remain responsive to societal demands.

There is a wealth of theoretical and descriptive literature, if not so many research studies, and my review is, of necessity, selective. Thus, opinions offered are, to some extent, personal and conclusions tentative. On the other hand, the range of themes detected and the frequency of their recurrence enables me to suggest that the review is at least representative of what has been written on the subject.

PATIENT PARTICIPATION DEFINED

There are a number of recurrent and overlapping themes detectable in the literature, but no clear consensus on what constitutes patient participation (Greenfield et al, 1985).

McEwen (1985) notes that allied terms such as 'self-help', 'demystification' and 'consumer participation' mean different things to different people and tend to have emotive connotations. He regards 'participation' as a more comprehensive concept, and uses it to describe the process whereby a person can function on his or her own behalf in the maintenance and promotion of health, the prevention of disease, the detection, treatment and care of illness, and adaptation to continuing disability. Participation may occur independently of, or within, the existing system of care, and extends to activities performed by individuals on behalf of others (e.g. family participation) and in the planning, management and evaluation of health-care provision. The following components of participation can be distinguished:

- *self-help*: active patient involvement in care;
- *demedicalisation or deprofessionalisation*: substitution of lay for professional care;

- *democratisation*: involvement of consumers in social policy decisions in the field of health care.

Many authors use the term 'self-care' to mean almost the same as 'patient participation'. For instance, Levin (1981) sees self-care as the process whereby patients deliberately act on their own behalf in health promotion, prevention of illness, and disease detection and treatment at the level of the primary health resource in the health-care system. Williamson and Danaher (1978) conceptualise self-care as a bimodal phenomenon, comprising health maintenance and the care of self in illness. Green and Moore (1980) divide self-care into three distinct areas:

1. symptom-related self-care for acute problems;
2. symptom-related self-care for chronic problems;
3. asymptomatic self-care involving alteration of life-style and risk factors.

Compared to the definition of participation above, self-care is, perhaps, a narrower concept more akin to McEwen's 'self-help'.

Nursing theorists have adopted the concept of self-care in constructing models and defining the role of the nurse. The person most commonly associated with the integration of self-care into nursing theory and practice is Dorothea Orem (1985). Orem believes that self-care is a learned, deliberate behaviour that people perform to meet and maintain certain specific needs (self-care requisites), such as the need for exercise, pain control, relaxation, air, food, and water. Such a broad interpretation of self-care may be very useful in encouraging nurses to place primary emphasis on the patient's own ability to attain and maintain health, but it tends to obscure the more radical connotations of participation, in which a reduced professional presence is envisaged.

The 'participating' patient has also been called the 'active' patient (e.g. Martin, 1978) or the 'activated patient' (Sehnert and Eisenberg, 1975), but it is evident that participants in the health-care process need not be 'patients' at all. For the purposes of this review terms will be used as follows:

- *Consumer*: a user, or potential user, of health-care services; the consumer may be a client or a patient (see below), or a member of the client or patient's family.
- *Client*: a consumer with no existing health-care problem; most

commonly the receiver of, or target for, health education and other forms of preventive health care.

- *Patient*: a consumer with an identified health deficit who has a relationship with a health-care provider for the purpose of receiving health-care services.
- *Health-care provider or professional*: a person who provides health-care services to patients, clients and their families as part of the officially recognised health service.

Although participation by consumers in general will be considered in the introductory and concluding sections of this account, the main emphasis, particularly in reviewing research, will be on the individual patient and his or her family. The concept of 'participation' adopted is that of Brownlea (1987):

> 'Participation means getting involved or being allowed to become involved in a decision-making process or the delivery of a service or the evaluation of a service, or even simply to become one of a number of people consulted on an issue or a matter.'

The value of such a loose definition lies in its acknowledgement of participation as a collaborative process, necessitating derogation of power by professionals and policy-makers.

THE VALUE OF PATIENT PARTICIPATION

Participation is widely regarded as 'a good thing':

> 'Positive health comes through participation and action, not through passive acceptance or "being a good patient".' (McCarthy, 1985)

Brownlea (1987) suggests that there may be value simply in participating, irrespective of the effect on outcome.

McEwen et al (1983) list the supposed advantages of greater consumer involvement in care, especially self-care:

- increased patient responsibility and commitment to health and health-promoting behaviours and activities;
- the contribution to health of new community-based resources, provided as a result of consumer demand;
- development of a new ecological concept of health;
- improved integration of existing health services, combined with better utilisation.

These supposed advantages have to be weighed against the following risks:

- possible increased delay in seeking care;
- ill-effects of self-diagnosis and self-medication;
- risks of conflicting advice;
- the danger of uncontrolled and unevaluated treatment;
- the misuse of highly technical information;
- alienation of professionals.

The risks and advantages of change have to be compared with those of the present system.

McEwen and his colleagues assert that participation in health 'is likely to be one of the major determinants of the health of our communities and the type of care that will be provided', and such a view is widely held. However, other authors note the lack of evaluative research to support this position (Brooking, 1986; Batehup, 1987).

Pritchard (1986) asks the question 'Why participate at all?', and identifies a range of advantages from doing so. In particular, consumers gain a sense of contribution and a feeling of some power or place in the system. The community gains in terms of the wider dissemination of health information and of playing a part in the negotiated approach to the allocation of resources. The doctor's role is extended and his aims clarified, thereby potentially enhancing the doctor–client relationship. The practice of medical care is improved as participation provides feedback from consumers to health-care staff, improves communication and job satisfaction and minimises the number of complaints. At the central level, participation lessens professional and technical domination of health care, helps the bureaucracy to respond to change and brings about a more appropriate allocation of resources, particularly when these resources are scarce.

In addition, sophisticated health services have tended to sap people's confidence in their ability to look after their own health (Illich, 1974). Participation may restore that confidence (Player, 1983).

DEVELOPMENT OF THE CONCEPT OF PATIENT PARTICIPATION

Participation was singled out as an essential component of progress in health care by a World Health Organisation (WHO)

Expert Committee on Health Education as long ago as 1953 (see Mahler, 1982). A number of disciplines has contributed to the development of the concept of patient participation and of the broader concept of community participation. I shall discuss the subject from social–historical, ethical and psychological perspectives.

Social–historical perspective

Steele et al (1987) suggest that the active patient concept has waxed and waned over the last two centuries in synchrony with broader societal change.

An aspect of consumerism

Terms such as 'consumer', 'provider', etc. are culled directly from the vocabulary of consumerism. The idea of consumer participation in publicly provided services, such as environmental planning, education and housing, became popular in the late 1960s and has been so ever since. Consequently, it is not surprising that in the area of health, also, attention has been directed towards finding the means of achieving greater consumer input (Richardson, 1983).

However, this does not entirely explain why consumer involvement became so 'fashionable' when it did. Richardson and Bray (1987) attribute this to a combination of consumers' increasing interest in service provision (paralleling consumer interest in other aspects of consumption) and the search by service providers for ways in which to engage with consumers. They admit that the general phenomenon of consumerism has played a role in the development of participatory mechanisms in the health field, but suggest that this provided a climate ripe for other influences to operate, rather than being itself the principal impetus.

In addition to *participation*, consumerism calls for some degree of *protection* for consumers. Ian Kennedy (1981) considers that consumerism is best understood as being concerned with protecting the legitimate concerns of the consumer in the face of the greater power of others to hurt, injure or exploit him, or to undermine his power of self-determination and responsibility for his own destiny. Consumerism's aim is for a better balance of power, in the light of prevailing values.

A consumerist stance can be seen as a challenge to professional authority, since it focuses on consumers' rights and providers' obligations rather than on the professional right to direct and patient obligation to comply (Haug and Lavin, 1981). It also presupposes that the consumer is competent to judge the quality of the product offered (Haug, 1980).

Changing professional – patient relationships

Starr (1982) traces the origins of the active patient concept from the move towards increasing personal freedom in the mid-eighteenth century. The call for more freedom in health was often associated with dissent in religious practice; for instance, the Methodist preacher, John Wesley, published a popular tract, *Primitive Physic*, which was critical of the mystification of medical care and accused doctors of distancing themselves from their patients.

Woodward and Richards (1977) describe the situation in nineteenth-century England, where traditional folk medicine and mutual self-help flourished. During this period, an extensive range of books and pamphlets was published on all aspects of health. In the latter half of the century there were two important portents of change in the doctor–patient relationship:

- Practitioners became more highly organised, and legislation was introduced, limiting who might practise as a healer (Bowling, 1981).
- Advances in medical science greatly increased the technical component of medicine. These included the introduction of antisepsis, the discovery of X-rays and anaesthesia, and the identification of the microorganisms causing cholera, diphtheria and tuberculosis (Reiser, 1978).

These developments heralded what Starr has termed 'the retreat of private judgement', a process accelerated in the early twentieth century by the discovery of vaccines, sera and effective drugs for a variety of conditions. The medical profession gradually increased in knowledge and power, and their sphere of influence widened as health services became more comprehensive and freely available (McKeown, 1965).

Broad social changes since the Second World War, for instance the rise in existentialist philosophy and vociferous calls for self-determination from groups such as ethnic minorities and women, have encouraged mistrust of authority and doubts about the benefits to be derived from technological advance (Thomasma, 1983). Correspondingly, emphasis in descriptions of the patient–provider relationship has shifted from deference to professional expertise and patient passivity towards the inclusion of more active patient involvement (Benarde and Mayerson, 1978; Brody, 1980).

Since the early 1970s, what Powles (1973) refers to as 'the crisis of contemporary professionalism' has become increasingly evident. Consumers have criticised the bureaucracy, inflexibility and impersonal nature of the health service, and recognition has grown that medicine cannot provide all the answers to the problems of living. Evidence of the negative consequences of professional care and of deficiencies in the rigorous evaluation of medical technology is causing a general re-assessment of the professional role in health care (Levin, 1981). The concept of 'iatrogenesis' has been developed by Illich (1974) and others, and the argument has been put forward that the only answer for medical 'mistakes' (e.g. vaccine-damaged children, thalidomide babies, etc.) is for the patient to be fully involved in the decision-making process.

Martini (1981) writes:

'The principal impetus for the steady growth of the self-care movement has been not so much the demonstrated efficacy of self-care as the crisis of confidence in professional medicine.'

Recent British figures show that the number of claims for negligence has increased eight times since the mid-1970s and is still rising. During 1988 health authorities in England will probably pay out £13m in legal fees and compensation to patients (Timmins, 1988).

Impetus for a change in patient–provider relationships has also come from the allied professions, such as nurses and psychologists. Engaged in their own struggles against hegemony, they have championed ideas of patient autonomy and have developed educational programmes and behavioural treatments designed to facilitate greater patient involvement (Steele et al, 1987).

Demographic and epidemiological factors
The pioneering work of Edwin Chadwick (see Flinn, 1965) laid the foundations of the public health movement in Britain, which had

a profound influence on morbidity and mortality (McKeown, 1965). The reduced burden of communicable and acute illness made more apparent the existence of a variety of chronic conditions (Fry, 1966). Sophisticated medical technology has increased the pool of chronic ill health by adding the survivors of ischaemic heart disease, diabetes, stroke, etc. (Barsky, 1976). This well-monitored shift from acute to chronic health problems is one factor in the rise of patient participation (McEwen et al, 1983).

Several characteristics of chronic illness are thought to make participation particularly appropriate:

- The present state of medical knowledge cannot offer a cure.
- Continuing care is needed, and although there is some degree of chronic impairment, this can be minimised and its effects mitigated if rehabilitation procedures are followed.
- Self-help has the potential to create a bond between sufferers and relatives, reducing the need for professional intervention.
- Group activities with other sufferers can provide the most appropriate practical help and emotional support.

Demographic changes have produced a marked increase in the proportion of elderly people in the population (Donaldson et al, 1983). Some suffer from chronic degenerative diseases, others are merely frail. In a way, dependent old age shares the characteristics of chronic disease listed above, and self-care can reduce the need for professional support.

Certain social and psychosocial changes, such as the weakening of traditional structures, alienation and loneliness, can manifest themselves as mental or physical ill health (Brown and Harris, 1978). This again leads to increased demand on the health service (World Health Organisation, 1976). Self-help may provide effective compensation for lack of social support.

Economic aspects
It has been suggested that Fry's 'insoluble equation' in health care (1979), whereby:

$$Wants > Needs > Resources$$

can be alleviated by more patient participation (Pistorius, 1983). A well-informed and motivated patient should know which ailments to manage himself, instead of exerting inappropriate pressure for professional care.

Community care is thought to be less expensive than institutional care, and *self*-care in the community should prove to be even cheaper (Griffiths, 1988). In the case of chronic illness most care takes place in the community anyway (Conrad, 1985), but increased patient participation may provide a substantial saving on scarce resources.

The trend towards private health-care provision can also have a positive effect on consumer involvement in an effort to reduce the cost of ill health. Berg and LoGerfo (1979) cite instances of health insurance companies in the USA sending self-help manuals to their subscribers in an attempt to reduce the number of claims. The British United Provident Association (BUPA), a non-profit-making health insurance company, has compiled its own health-care manual for consumers (BUPA, 1984), 'emphasizing self-help, self-motivation, safety and common sense'.

International aspect

Developments in Europe and the USA can be viewed as part of a worldwide movement to promote community participation in health care. An international conference in the USSR resulted in the Declaration of Alma-Ata (World Health Organisation, 1978), which states:

> 'The people have the right and duty to participate individually and collectively in the planning and implementation of their health care. This is clearly a basic human right and is supported by current ideas on the nature of health and illness. Health can never be adequately protected by health services without the active understanding and involvement of the individuals and communities whose health is at stake. Action to promote health therefore depends on a partnership, based on mutual understanding and trust, between those working in the health sector and the community.'

Pritchard (1986) regards the message of Alma-Ata as reinforcement for a pre-existent tide of popular demand for greater involvement, and as a challenge for the future.

Communities have become increasingly aware of two important facts (Brownlea, 1987):

- Many health problems are environment and life-style related;
- Medically oriented health-care systems have limited capacity and limited impact, and they are expensive to operate.

Community involvement is expected to be cost-effective and, more importantly, to be the best way of providing comprehensive solutions to public health problems (Madan, 1987). It forms the basis of WHO's Primary Health Care Strategy for achieving 'Health for All by the Year 2000' (World Health Organisation, 1981).

Participation in health is linked to other forms of community development. For instance, it has been described as a 'lever' (Mahler, 1983) or a 'wedge' (MacDonald, 1983), providing motivation and improved physical and mental ability for the accomplishment of other social reforms.

Ethical perspective

The main ethical principles raised in a discussion of patient participation are usually those of *autonomy, paternalism, non-maleficence* and *beneficence*. Many definitions of these terms exist. Childress (1979) defines paternalism as an action taken by one person in the best interests of another *without* the latter's consent, whereas Thomasma (1983) wishes to distinguish between 'strong' paternalism and 'weak' paternalism. Strong paternalism is exercised against the wishes of another; weak paternalism is an action taken by a physician in the best interests of a patient on presumed wishes, or in the absence of consent for those who cannot give consent due to age or mental status. In some instances, weak paternalism is practised when a doctor ascertains the best course of action ahead of time and presents only this option to the competent patient. 'Autonomy' stems from the Greek for 'self-law or rule': a person is regarded as possessing basic human rights, which include the right to self-determination (Dyer and Bloch, 1987).

Sociological studies (e.g. Freidson, 1970a) suggest that one of the identifying features of a profession is a considerable degree of autonomy. The 'sick role' (Parsons, 1951) places patients in a passive, dependent position where decision-making is left to the doctor. Thus, a medically dominated health-care system tends to be characterised by professional autonomy and paternalism – albeit beneficent (Ingelfinger, 1980; Thomasma, 1983). There have been calls for increased *patient* autonomy in recent years, notably in the areas of informed consent, the rights of the mentally ill (Gostin, 1983) and in women's health, particularly related to childbirth (e.g. *Who's Having your Baby?*, Beech, 1988). The argument can also be extended to patients' rights to participate in all aspects of their care. Cassell (1976) goes so far as to suggest that the primary aim of health care should be restoration of patient autonomy rather than cure or restoration of function. Ethical aspects will be considered in more detail later, in relation to the concept of informed consent.

Psychological perspective

Psychological theory has tended to support the contention that increased participation in health care is likely to prove beneficial to patients, but with a number of reservations.

Most arguments centre on the issue of 'control' and derive from social learning theory (Bandura, 1977, 1986). This postulates that individuals interact with their environments in a reciprocal way; that is, environmental factors influence the behaviour of the individual and, at the same time, the individual has the capacity both to structure supportive environments and to resist environmental pressures (Cameron and Best, 1987). Relevant concepts are described below.

Locus of control

Locus of control 'refers to the degree to which an individual perceives events that happen to him/her as dependent on his/her own behaviour or as a result of luck, chance, fate, or powers (including other persons) beyond his/her control and understanding' (Strickland, 1978). In a new situation, an individual will depend on generalised expectations that have proved helpful in the past. The internal/external dimension to locus of control is a *generalised* expectancy that individuals bring to bear on all situations, the nature of the expectation depending on whether they feel that events are contingent (or not) on their behaviour. Rotter (1975) depicts a continuum, with persons who are inner-oriented placed at one end and those who feel externally controlled by the environment at the opposite end. Research suggests that individuals who believe that events are related to their own behaviour are more likely to take steps to modify adverse life situations (Strickland, 1965).

Self-efficacy

Self-efficacy theory proposes that 'people's perceptions of their capabilities affect how they behave, their level of motivation, their thought patterns, and their emotional reactions to taxing situations' (O'Leary, 1985). O'Leary sees enormous potential in behavioural medicine for assessing and enhancing self-perception of efficacy, and for utilising this to promote change in health behaviours, such as smoking cessation, weight control, etc. She visualises enhancing perceived self-efficacy by providing 'performance mastery experiences' to clients.

Learned helplessness

According to Seligman (1975), learned helplessness arises when an individual discovers that there is no response that can be made to alleviate or control an aversive stimulus. It is not the stimulus itself, but the lack of perceived control, that leads to passivity, feelings of helplessness and, possibly, depression (Beck, 1967). The incentive to respond to the aversive stimulus is undermined, and reduced motivation for response may be generalised to other stimuli.

Reactance

Psychological reactance (Brehm, 1966) is a reaction to loss of control that involves attempts to restore lost freedoms. Wortman and Brehm (1975) have attempted to integrate the model of learned helplessness with reactance theory. In this view, the initial reaction to loss of control is resistance (i.e. reactance), which is replaced by compliance (i.e. helplessness) if control fails to be restored over time.

Relating these concepts to the theme of patient participation, Krantz et al (1980) write:

> 'Heightened participation and choice often lead to increases in perceived control, since they may provide subjects with the belief (correct or not) that they can alter or affect outcome.'

There is a need here to distinguish between control over process (means) and control over outcomes (ends). A substantial body of evidence now supports the idea that 'choice aids recovery' (e.g. Hames and Stirling, 1987). However, Smith et al (1984) suggest that, although control over processes may be motivated by a desire to control outcomes, controlling the process may be a desirable goal in itself.

Attempting to summarise this argument:

- Patient participation increases feelings of control, but this perception may be illusory (Krantz et al).
- Effective control of process (participating in care) may be beneficial in itself, regardless of outcome (Smith et al).
- Effective patient involvement in decision-making can improve outcome also (Hames and Stirling).

From this formulation, one potential problem becomes obvious: if patients' initial perceptions of control prove to have no effect on process or outcome, this may have a negative effect on self-efficacy, contribute to learned helplessness, or cause a shift towards a more external locus of control. (This is of relevance to patient participation in chronic illness, as discussed in chapter 3.) Conversely, a positive experience of control through participation may enhance self-efficacy and comprises, in O'Leary's terms, a performance mastery experience. This, in turn, may contribute to the patients' success in changing their own health behaviour.

Information has also been conceptualised as a form of *cognitive* control (Averill, 1973; Janis and Rodin, 1979), because it may increase the ability to prepare for aversive events and can result in the interpretation of events in a way that lessens perceived threat (Seligman, 1975). Knowing in advance about an event (predictability) is usually necessary in order to have control over it, but, in the absence of control, predictability alone may be of some value (Schulz, 1976).

Desire for control of health care can be seen, therefore, as a preference for behaviours which:

- allow direct influence on the process of care;
- provide relevant information about the health-care situation; or
- do both. (Smith et al, 1984)

Desire for control is aimed at 'coping', defined by Lazarus and Launier (1978) as consisting of both cognitive and behavioural efforts aimed at mastering a stressful transaction. They emphasise that coping efforts can be focused either on dealing with the problem itself or on managing the unpleasant emotions that are aroused because of the problem.

Summary

The above section has described some of the factors instrumental in the development of the concept of patient participation. At the macro-level these factors are well summarised by Hickey (1986):

- increasing consumer knowledge, assisted by the media;
- increasing awareness of consumer rights;
- a general move towards all forms of self-help;
- acceleration of health-care costs and economic stringency;
- increasing awareness of the fallibility of health professionals.

Mention has also been made of the increasing proportion of elderly, disabled and chronically ill in the population, for whom participation might be especially appropriate. Hickey makes a further important point that, as far as self-care is based in the community, its development can be interpreted as a reaction to the dominance of the institution in the health-care system.

At the level of the individual patient and his family, participation has potentially beneficial psychological effects and is supported ethically to the extent that personal autonomy is enhanced. The relationship between the patient and the health-care provider has also undergone a change, towards a greater level of mutuality. This can be seen partly as a response to consumer pressure and also as a factor promoting further involvement in decision-making.

Although it is possible to chart the influence of broader movements of social change, new patterns of health and illness and the changing role of medicine and health-care professionals, it is difficult to assess, retrospectively, the relative contribution of each. Some views call for increased participation chiefly as a 'protective reaction' to a system that does not seem to be providing the kind of choices in health care that a community feels it needs (Brownlea, 1987). So, how much does the current movement represent a positive desire to participate fully in health decisions, and how much does it reflect criticisms of the quality and quantity of the professional service? This issue is raised by McEwen et al (1983), and they go on to pose two further questions of interest:

1. Is participation a logical extension of existing and widely practised self-care or is it a wish to experiment with new forms of health care?

2.   Is the aim to set up an alternative to existing services or to work with them to provide different or additional skills, care or advice?

It is important to ask such questions, but no clear-cut answers can be provided because, to return to my starting point, participation means different things to different people. Van den Heuvel (1980) stresses the need for conceptual clarification, specifically in the area of consumer involvement in health policy. However, conceptual clarity is difficult to achieve when, by the nature of participation, lay people, professionals and policy-makers interact. On the other hand, with good communication and an open acknowledgement of differing viewpoints, interaction can be a powerful stimulus for change and innovation. It also provides a testing ground for new concepts and a forum for critical appraisal of initiatives.

SOME INITIATIVES IN PATIENT PARTICIPATION

Without devoting too much space to the subject, this section describes a few interesting initiatives in consumer participation by government and health service management, health-care professionals and groups of consumers. Later sections will examine in more detail participation in the individual patient-provider interaction.

Health service management and government

Consumer consultation and policy decisions
Richardson and Bray (1987) write:

> '. . . policy makers have increasingly acknowledged the importance of the consumer view and the need for consumers to play a growing role in service planning.'

Evidence of this acknowledgement appears in a number of policy documents, for instance the Cumberlege Report (Department of Health and Social Security, 1986a) and the government discussion document on Primary Health Care (Department of Health and Social Security, 1986b):

> 'If health authorities and health professionals are to take the interests of the consumer seriously, there needs to be a forum where local

people can contribute their views on health needs and health care planning.' (Cumberlege Report)

'individual members of the public as recipients of services are often better placed to judge the quality of delivery of services than the NHS bodies responsible for them.' (Government discussion document)

Of course, homage to consumer involvement could be regarded as purely political rhetoric. This is particularly the case in the latter document, which calls for contributions to the discussion on primary health care, while simultaneously precluding from the agenda important issues raised by Cumberlege, such as a proposal to change the independent contractor status of general practitioners. Locker and Dunt (1978) state that 'studies of consumer opinion, *to the extent that they are taken into account in policy formulations*, are an indirect form of consumer participation' (emphasis added).

The National Association for Mental Health (MIND) played a significant part in getting the 1983 Mental Health Act onto the Statute Books (Hoggett, 1984). The Act is widely acknowledged as a major improvement over the 1959 Act (Brooking, 1984), but change took over 20 years to effect. How much eventual success can be owed to increased government willingness to acknowledge consumer opinion is open to debate.

Community health councils

Community health councils (CHCs) were introduced following the 1974 reorganisation of the National Health Service (NHS) to provide a formal and statutory mechanism for the consumer voice (Richardson and Bray, 1987). They have three broad functions: providing individual help and advice to consumers, representation of consumer interests at meetings of the health authority (although they have no voting rights), and health education. The effectiveness of CHCs has been questioned on several fronts; for example, they have limited access to information, commitment of members varies from council to council, and they are probably not representative of consumers as a whole (Levitt, 1980).

Health service ombudsman

The office of the Health Service Commissioner, or Ombudsman, was also introduced in 1974. The Commissioner has an independent role and receives complaints about any aspect of NHS care and management, except those relating to clinical judgments. In addition, complaints will only be investigated if no legal action is planned, and providing the complaint is made within a year of the incident involved. Complaints must be made to the authority concerned in the first instance (Office of Health Economics, 1984).

Health-care professionals

Health promotion

The World Health Organisation (1984) has defined health promotion as 'the process of enabling people to increase control over, and to improve, their health'. This involves seeking to actively engage consumers in prevention and health education. The same document continues: 'health promotion aims particularly at effective and concrete public participation'.

Others take a more cynical view of health promotion. For instance, Williams (1984) contrasts it unfavourably with health education. Two central goals of health education are rational decision-making and personal autonomy, whereas health promotion involves 'the hard sell':

> 'Promotion is about convincing other people that they need, or ought to have, what the salesman or promoter wants them to have.'

Patient participation groups in general practice

The first patient participation group was started in 1972, and, at the last count, there were nearly 100 in existence (Pritchard, 1988). Usually the groups consist of patients, doctors and staff associated with a particular practice or health centre. In most instances, they are started on the initiative of the general practitioners (GPs) themselves. The activities of groups vary enormously, but their general aims are to improve the effectiveness of the practice, to provide complementary voluntary services, and to foster health education and preventive care (Richardson and Bray, 1987). Wood and Metcalfe (1980) claim that patient participation groups do increase the effectiveness of the practice, improve doctor-patient relationships and extend the role of the GP.

Some doctors have reservations about the value of patient participation groups. For example, Kerrigan (1983) writes:

> 'It is not enough for doctors to encourage their patients to take a more

active role in managing their own illnesses, which is a laudable concept; there is now a move to encourage patients to take a greater part in the management of other people's illnesses.'

Kerrigan is also concerned about the representativeness of the people who become involved, and Coleman (1986) suggests that the doctors who are prepared to listen to patient representatives are the ones who least need advice.

Self-care guides

There are a number of publications on the market, often written by health-care professionals but designed to promote self-care and/or more appropriate use of the health service. Examples directed at a general audience include *The Sunday Times Book of Body Maintenance* (Gillie and Mercer, 1982), *The Health Care Manual: A Family Guide to Self-Care and Home Medicines* (Fry and Fryers, 1983) and *The Patient's Companion: How to Get Good Health Care* (Coleman, 1986). There is also an extensive range of material for more specialised groups, such as pregnant women, those with chronic back pain, etc.

Consumers

Self-help groups

A large number of self-help groups has appeared in recent years, and these have provided a fruitful field for study. The groups have focused on an ever-widening range of medical (and other) conditions. Katz and Bender (1976) provide a useful general definition:

> 'Self-help groups are voluntary, small group structures for mutual aid and the accomplishment of a special purpose. They are usually founded by peers who have come together for mutual assistance in satisfying a common need, overcoming a common handicap or life-disrupting problem and bringing about desired social and/or personal change.'

There may be considerable input from health professionals in the form of skill- and knowledge-sharing.

Some groups have developed because of shortfalls in the amount or quality of help available from existing services in the local community. Sometimes self-help health-care groups are used as referral resources for professionals (Brownlea, 1987). Gartner and Reissman (1976) have suggested that self-help groups are the key to planning for management of chronic diseases. Certainly, there is growing professional interest in these groups and the possibility of working with them (Richardson, 1984).

Health Help 1987/88 (Duin and Jacka, 1987), produced for Thames Television's 'Help!' programme as 'A guide to organisations that can help you with your health problems', lists more than 700 such organisations, from national bodies and advice services to informal self-help groups.

The women's health movement

The concept of women's health as a discrete, political phenomenon originated in the USA in the later 1960s (Martin, 1978), and can be seen as the fusion of two social movements: health consumerism and the women's liberation movement (McEwen et al, 1983). Probably the most influential publication in the field has been *Our Bodies, Ourselves* (Boston Women's Health Book Collective, 1971; Rakusen and Phillips, 1978 [revised British version]), although there has been a rapid escalation in the volume of literature concerned with women's health. Ehrenreich and English (1979) have documented the history of the movement and link it to the position of women as important providers of health care. Abortion, the medicalisation of pregnancy and childbirth, and gynaecological self-help continue to be prominent issues, but much has also been accomplished in health education and consciousness-raising about the wider aspects of women's health.

Community health initiatives

There is a variety of other local organisations concerned with health needs, including community development projects and community health groups. The National Community Health Resource (formerly the Community Health Initiatives Resource Unit and the London Community Health Resource) produces a quarterly magazine *Community Health Action*, and has recently published a book, *Guide to Community Health Projects* (CHIRU/ LCHR, 1987). It runs training courses for community health workers and is active in a variety of campaigns, for example, improving racial equality in health care and drawing attention to the health needs of the homeless.

The Patients' Association is a national voluntary organisation, set up in 1963, to promote the interests of patients in their dealings with the NHS.

THE PROFESSIONAL RESPONSE

The patient – provider relationship has changed over the last 20 years, and health-care workers have initiated or supported schemes to promote patient involvement in service provision and self-help (see above). As already noted, it is difficult to assess to what extent professional attitudes and behaviours are a *response* to broader social change and, more specifically, consumer calls for participation, and how much they provide the *impetus* for change. Accepting that the movement gained initial momentum from the desire of (some) consumers and (some) professionals for greater engagement in care, it seems clear that this movement subsequently called forth from professional groups a variety of responses, both reactionary and progressive. From the literature several themes emerge. A brief examination of these themes may be of value in elucidating the ideologies influencing research.

The medical response

Participation as a challenge to physician authority
While there is widespread recognition of the patient's right to autonomy, this often sits uncomfortably with doctors' perceptions of their role. Brody (1980) admits that doctors may be reluctant to relinquish their power and control over patients. For some, maintaining power and authority is a goal in itself; others view the potential loss of autonomy as a threat to their professional status and appearance of competency (Freidson, 1970a, b). Freidson (1970a) summarises this attitude by stating:

> 'in any profession one working definition of success is the attainment of such prestige that one need not deal with anyone who does not come in as a humble supplicant eager to obey; it is the young practitioner and the comparative failure who must cope with questioning.'

Perhaps this is an extreme view, or less true now than when it was written, but the call for more patient participation does elicit a protective response from some quarters. Fry (1983) suggests that doctors will have to be convinced that participation is beneficial not only for the patients but also for themselves. It is certainly seen as beneficial in its potential for reducing inappropriate consultations and the burden of 'trivia' (Williamson and Danaher,

1978). As indicated by the results of a symposium, published by the *British Medical Journal* in 1978 (Avery-Jones, 1978; Smith, 1978), some doctors see the answers to problems in the health service in terms of strict demarcation of the contributions of government, professionals and public, with few areas of overlap.

More radical medical opinion actively encourages patients to challenge their doctors (e.g. Sehnert and Eisenbert, 1975; Dawson, 1983) and expresses its willingness to respond positively to such an approach (e.g. Pritchard, 1983). Perhaps the most frequent attitude is a qualified acceptance, as described by Quill (1983). Many doctors are starting to re-examine their relationships with patients, and are experimenting with other types of care while seeking to retain 'the strengths of traditional medical care'. These strengths are not specified by Quill, but the following paragraphs suggest some aspects of their traditional role that doctors hold particularly dear.

The competence gap

As Haug and Lavin (1981) note, any level of patient consumerism implies a belief in a narrowed competence gap between the patient and professional. Szasz and Hollender (1956) recognised that varying levels of involvement might be appropriate for different categories of patient. They see the 'activity – passivity' model as entirely appropriate for the treatment of emergencies (e.g. for the patient who is severely injured, bleeding, delirious or unconscious). The model of 'guidance – cooperation' is suggested for those who are less ill than the first group, but who suffer from distressing symptoms (e.g. pain, anxiety or symptoms of acute infection). These patients require treatment and will probably be willing to place the physician in a position of some power. 'Mutual participation' is only advocated for the management of chronic illnesses (e.g. diabetes mellitus, chronic heart disease), although Szasz and Hollender note that it may be favoured unrealistically by patients who want to take care of themselves as an 'over-compensatory attempt at mastering anxieties associated with helplessness and passivity'.

Since Szasz and Hollender formulated their scheme 30 years ago, mutual participation has gained credibility as a more general approach. However, worries are expressed about the ability and/or willingness of patients to become involved at various points in the health-care process. There is, for example, a long-running debate about the advisability or otherwise of allowing patients access to their medical records (e.g. *British Medical Journal*, 1986).

Also on the theme of information, the courts have been involved in deciding what constitutes 'relevant' information for informed consent (Dyer and Bloch, 1987). In some states in the USA the law has stipulated that consent can be regarded as informed only when the 'prudent patient' test is satisfied; that is, the 'reasonable patient' is informed about all material risk involved in the proposed treatment to which he or she would probably attach significance in coming to a decision on whether or not to forego the proposed treatment. English law has adopted a quite different position. In the case *Sidaway* v. *Bethlem Royal Hospital* (1984) the doctor was discharging his duty reasonably if he acted in accordance with clinical practice 'rightly accepted by a body of skilled and experienced medical men'. Dyer and Bloch quote from the case's conclusion:

> 'The evidence in this case showed that a contrary result would be damaging to the relationship of trust and confidence between doctor and patient, and might well have an adverse effect on the practice of medicine. It is doubtful whether it would be of any significant benefit to patients, most of whom prefer to put themselves unreservedly in the hand of their doctors.'

It would seem, in this instance, that many doctors are more enlightened than the law about the amount of involvement patients wish to have and their competence to participate in decision-making. However, McCall Smith's remark (1977) is probably worth bearing in mind:

> 'the law may ultimately be called upon to define what is acceptable practice on the part of the professions but it tends to do so on the basis of what the professions themselves suggest.'

Levin (1981) notes widespread professional concern about the safety of self-care practices, including self-medication. However, compared to the literature on the dangers of professional care, there is little to suggest that self-care is any more ineffective or hazardous. In fact, the few studies available suggest that self-care practices before professional help is sought are 'overwhelmingly safe and appropriate'.

The competency of patients to evaluate care has also been called into question. Indeed, there is a tendency for patients to express high levels of satisfaction with service provision and treatment received (Locker and Dunt, 1978; Speedling and Rose, 1985), and there does seem to be some justification for Marsh and Kaim-Caudle's observation (1976) that respondents are not able to assess properly the quality of the treatment received nor the quantity they need. This situation leads the authors to conclude:

> 'As patients are not able to judge the quality of the service they receive nor the quantity of the care they require it seems quite legitimate and proper to set out deliberately to persuade them to want what is in their own best interest and what can be provided efficiently.'

Fortunately, this view is balanced by that of professionals who see the answer in terms of reducing the competence gap through greater patient involvement in care (e.g. Brownlea et al, 1980).

Compliance

Some authorities consider that the problem of enlisting patient cooperation with treatment is 'the most serious challenge facing medical practice today' (Janz et al, 1984). Dracup and Meleis (1982) define compliance as the extent to which an individual chooses behaviours that coincide with clinical prescription. Non-compliance describes behaviours that vary from the prescribed regimen. The language of compliance and non-compliance sometimes carries overtones of religious attitudes to sin; for example, Dracup and Meleis distinguish two types of non-compliant behaviour: 'behaviours of omission and behaviours of commission'. Benarde and Mayerson (1978) suggest that conflict exists between the doctor, who wishes to have his patient follow directions exactly, and the patient, 'who wishes to get away with as little as possible and still maintain his health'.

Apparently measurement of compliance is no easy matter. Roth (1987) provides a 'rule of thumb':

> 'The cheapest and simplest method for determining whether a patient has taken his medicine is to ask him. If the patient answers that he did not, this is probably true. If, however, the patient answers that he took the medication as directed, but it is important for the doctor to know whether the medicine was taken as prescribed, then this answer must be accepted with caution.'

He goes on to suggest that research priority should be given to the development of simple, easily performed and inexpensive methods for measuring blood or urine levels of medications and their metabolites.

Stimson (1974) was one of the first to draw attention to the fact that patients may have their own very good and rational reasons for not obeying doctors' orders. Conrad (1985) has elaborated on these reasons in research on patients with epilepsy. In his view, the regulation of medications is one way in which people struggle to gain some personal control over their condition and some freedom from those who 'push' them to adhere to a particular medication practice. Ross's review of compliance and her research (1987) draw attention to many important aspects of compliance, in particular the rationality of non-compliance from the patient's perspective and the phenomenon of 'professional non-compliance', that is, failure to follow recognised practice.

As Stimson notes, it is an unquestioned assumption in many studies that the patient should comply: the doctor knows best and the patient is to be passive, obedient and unquestioning. Non-compliance is deemed to be a form of deviance, in need of explanation (Parsons, 1951). Compliance differs markedly from most conceptualisations of participation or self-care as the latter emphasise the patient's role as decision-maker (McIntyre, 1980). In spite of this, many researchers have defined patient participation purely in terms of compliance with treatment decided by the doctor (Greenfield et al, 1985).

Benarde and Mayerson observed in 1978 that, although the number of publications concerned with non-compliance had increased sharply over the previous decade, they were 'unaware of any that propose ways to increase patient compliance'. Having spent some time searching the literature for studies relating to patient participation, I can state that this is no longer the case. Wilson-Barnett and Osborne (1983), for example, review patient teaching studies, some of which are aimed at improving compliance. Other examples will be discussed in a later section. I agree with Greenfield and colleagues: patient participation continues to be interpreted by researchers as compliance. However, there is growing recognition that patients can and should participate in the formulation of the treatment plan.

The provider – patient dyad

> 'We defined patient involvement in care within the context of the physician – patient interaction, because it is there that patients can have the greatest impact on medical decisions and the course of treatment.' (Greenfield et al, 1985)

Much attention has been paid in recent years to attempts to improve the quality of the doctor – patient relationship, and rightly so. Cartwright and O'Brien found in 1976 that doctors were more satisfied with consultations lasting fewer than 5 minutes, in which the patient asked no more than one question and when few problems were discussed. On the other hand, patients are more satisfied with an encounter if given a chance to talk, and compliance improves as a result (Putnam et al, 1985).

Since Szasz and Hollender's early contribution, many alternative conceptualisations of doctor – patient interaction have been put foward; including:

- the contractual approach (e.g. Quill, 1983);
- patient – physician negotiation (e.g. Benarde and Mayerson, 1978; Eisenthal et al, 1979);
- the customer approach (e.g. Lazare et al, 1975);
- the fiduciary principle (e.g. Dyer and Bloch, 1987).

To some extent, these represent different aspects of a basically similar approach rather than discrete models. The emphasis is on partnership and shared responsibility:

> 'Negotiation is a process where two active and equal participants negotiate to obtain their respective goals (which are often at odds).' (Benarde and Mayerson, 1978)

Concern to improve communication is commendable, and is intimately related to the concept of patient participation. Unfortunately, much of the literature in this area tends to overlook fundamental inequalities in the relationship. Stimson and Webb (1975), among others, describe territorial, social, cultural and educational barriers to effective communication. Such barriers lead to an imbalance of power, which leaves the patient in a weakened bargaining position.

In addition, there is a potential disadvantage in channelling so much energy into reforming the one-to-one relationship with a professional: it may divert attention from the more fundamental social and political changes that are required if participation is to become a reality (Versluyen, 1976).

The nursing response

The role of the nurse
The definitions quoted below demonstrate that nurse leaders, at least, attach some importance to the concept of patient participation. In contrast to medicine, patient participation is seen not as a potential threat to the nurse's autonomy but as a positive part of her role. However, these statements raise a few potential difficulties which require comment.

1. Lambertson (1958) defines nursing as:

> 'a dynamic therapeutic and educative process in meeting the health needs of society ... assisting individuals and/or families to achieve a desirable degree of self-direction for health, depending upon their potential.'

What constitutes a desirable level of self-direction and how the patient's potential is to be assessed is open to question. Szasz and Hollender's work of the same period (1956), already mentioned, suggests that the model of mutual participation becomes more appropriate and necessary 'the greater the intellectual, educational, and general experiential similarity between physician and patient'. It is not easy to provide any more appropriate and objective criteria for determining a patient's optimal level of self-direction. However, nurses are making some progress in this direction, as will be discussed in chapter 3.

2. One of the most frequently quoted definitions of nursing is that of Virginia Henderson (1960, revised 1969):

> 'The unique function of the nurse is to assist the individual (sick or well) in the performance of those activities contributing to health or its recovery (or to peaceful death) that he would perform unaided if he had the necessary strength, will or knowledge. And to do this in such a way as to help him gain independence as rapidly as possible.'

The criterion for nursing intervention is lack of strength, will or knowledge, although the type of assistance to be supplied is not differentiated according to the specific deficit: nurses are not precluded from, say, offering physical assistance to meet a knowledge deficit. Of course, this may conflict with the goal of patient independence. Faced by the stroke patient who does not know how to dress himself, or seems apathetic or 'too slow', many nurses (and relatives) are tempted to take over (Batehup, 1987). Miller (1985) notes the assumption that nursing care is given in response to a patient's degree of incapacity. However, her study demonstrated that nursing care can actually produce dependency.

A valuable contribution by Henderson is her concept of nursing's independent role, being 'that part of their work which nurses initiate and control, and of which they are masters'. If doctors have control of most areas of health care and nurses have control of some others, one wonders how much scope this leaves for *patient* initiative and control of care.

3. Orem's self-care model has already been mentioned. Orem (1985) states that:

> 'The condition which validates the existence of a requirement for nursing in an adult is the absence of the ability to maintain for himself continuously that amount and quality of self-care which is therapeutic in sustaining life and health, in recovering from disease or injury, or in coping with their effects ... Self-care is an adult's personal, continuous contribution to his health and well-being.'

Melnyk (1983) has pointed out that Orem's theory relegates the nurse to the position of a substitute self-care agent. In Orem's scheme, health and illness are, in a sense, peripheral issues: they may give rise to a self-care deficit, but it is this deficit and not the illness that justifies nursing intervention.

4. Shetland (1965) describes nursing as a process which is:

> 'one of interaction. The nurse enters imaginatively and sensitively into the lives of the people she serves in order to understand their health needs, determine the perception of their needs, reconcile the difference between the two sets of perceptions and institute appropriate nursing measures in interaction with the recipient(s) of her service.'

This early statement directly acknowledges the partnership between nurse and provider in assessment, planning and implementation of care. It also recognises the tensions that may arise when perceptions of need differ.

Of course, definitions such as these are limited in their intent, and it is wrong to judge a theory merely on the basis of a single statement. Nevertheless, it is interesting to note how fundamental the concept of patient participation is to nurses' perception of their role. This can be viewed in an historical context. Mauksch and Miller (1981) see change in nursing as brought about by a combination of:

- societal demands;
- inter-professional expectations and demands;
- intra-professional decisions;
- an overall climate of change in society.

Nurses have been seeking to define their role in new ways at a time of growing consumer demand for involvement in health care. Williamson and Danaher (1978) state:

'The best option for an expanding nursing profession is to assimilate new developments in the health services which require professional supervision of some sort but which the medical profession seems to ignore.'

Patient participation can be seen as such a development. Others view the situation differently. For example, Oakley (1984) feels that much of what the consumer movement in health care has said, and continues to say, already has echoes in the history and ideology of nursing. Nursing does not have to 'cover its tracks' in order to respond appropriately and successfully to consumer demands; it has always associated itself with a caring and environmental model of health and illness.

The crisis of professionalism
Professionalism has been described as 'a form of imperialism' (Illich, 1973). The meaning of such a charge is well illustrated by McKnight's definition of professionalism (1977):

'We need to solve your problems.
We need to tell you what they are.
We need to deal with them in our terms.
We need to have you respect our satisfaction with our own work.'

As discussed in the case of medicine, the establishment of an occupation as a profession rests on several factors, one of which is the demonstration of a competence gap between members of the profession and the public. The reward for professionalisation is a considerable degree of autonomy.

Some authors (e.g. Oakley, 1984; Salvage, 1985) see a clear case for rejecting the lure of professional status: they regard the main strength of nursing as lying in the fact that nurses are not members of the professional power elite, whose authority is presently being challenged by consumers. Instead, they have an opportunity to reshape their place in health care so that they are more closely allied with their patients. Other writers (e.g. Clay, 1987) would argue that only through the achievement of professional status and, in particular, through improved educational preparation will nurses have the power, liberty, confidence and ability to develop their role as they choose. Greater autonomy for nursing from medical domination can be a way to greater autonomy for patients.

Members of an occupation often pursue an 'occupational strategy', that is, a coherent set of behaviours designed to 'improve' in some way the position of the occupational group as a whole (Davies, 1976). Sometimes that strategy is one of achieving control via the creation of a 'dependency advantage', but it is not invariably so. This seems to be the challenge to nursing in relation to patient participation: to improve occupational status, whether by professionalisation or otherwise, while simultaneously seeking to reduce rather than increase patient dependency.

The nurse as patient advocate

The concept of advocacy is an interesting one as it seems to highlight some of the ambiguities already observed in the nurse's role. Conway-Rutkowski (1982) states:

> 'As an approach for an individual is formulated, the nurse must be a covert and overt advocate for the patient and family, since their lack of knowledge and understanding often places them in a vulnerable position.'

Copp (1986) also describes nurse advocacy in terms of speaking for 'vulnerable persons'. As Copp admits, there is a continuum of vulnerability: anyone in contact with the health-care system could be described as vulnerable to some extent. However, if the nurse 'speaks for' the patient and his family, does this not undermine their right to independence and self-determination?

Dyer and Bloch (1987) have discussed this question with respect to the psychiatric patient. They see an irony in some of the protective safeguards offered by the Mental Health Act 1983 in that the paternalistic role of the psychiatrist is simply transferred to the MHA Commissioner 'or other patient's advocate'. This does not restore the patient's autonomy; it merely substitutes someone else as a spokesman for the patient.

It appears, therefore, that regarding people as 'vulnerable' may be unhelpful if this causes nurses to usurp patients' right to speak for themselves. Moughton (1982) goes some way towards resolving this dilemma when she suggests that, as an advocate, the nurse supports the decisions made by the patient even when she is not fully in agreement with them. If the patient has weighed the alternatives and understands the consequences, the nurse should accept the decision, unless it is likely to produce harmful results. So, in most cases, the nurse does not speak 'instead of' the patient but adds her voice to his or hers.

Good reasons have been put forward against nurses adopting the role of advocate, and these need to be seriously addressed. They include the following (Castledine, 1981):

- The nurse's unique role results in the patient being forced to be dependent on her, for fear of pain and suffering.
- The patient has little choice of who is to act as his advocate.
- Even if the nurse does act as advocate for this patient, she may not be able to do this independently of the constraints of the institution or the authority of the employer.
- The nurse's educational background may not prepare her for an effective advocacy role.

Nursing practice and research
Nursing theory accommodates the concept of patient participation. Nursing models (e.g. Roper et al, 1980) have patient independence as the goal of intervention. Is there any evidence that nurses are attempting to increase patient and family involvement in care? Certainly, descriptive accounts are available from nurses in various settings who are trying to make patient participation in the nursing process a reality (e.g. Wilding et al, 1988). As the recent work of Brooking (1986) and Batehup (1987) demonstrates, there are not only problems to be surmounted in this area, but also an enormous potential for development.

Research evidence to guide and support practice appears, at first sight, to be sparse and fragmentary. (The limited definition of 'patient' should be recalled; studies relating to 'clients' are more numerous.) When I first approached the subject, the studies that came to light seemed to reflect themes common to medical research. For instance, nurses have contributed to the work on patient compliance, mainly through studies of patient teaching and information-giving (Potter, 1981). The rational assumption made is that compliance decisions must be knowledge-based. However, there is some evidence of confusion about how compliance relates to active participation. (Marston [1976], for example, defines patient compliance as self-care behaviours undertaken by a person to promote health, prevent illness and follow recommendations for the treatment of illness.) Nurse researchers have also looked at ways to facilitate negotiation in the doctor − patient interaction, through studies of question-asking and pre-appointment patient 'coaching' (e.g. Roter, 1977).

Studies such as these are valuable, but they do not really address the possibilities and potential difficulties of patient participation in dimensions of care beyond patient − provider interaction and compliance with prescribed treatment. I suspected, however, that my initial judgment on the limited nature of nursing research in patient participation might be incorrect. The approach developed for chapter 3 of this account aims to uncover some aspects of nursing research less explicitly related to improving patient participation, but with the potential to make important contributions to practice in this area.

Summary

The last section of this chapter has examined some of the themes in the medical and nursing literature that are related to patient participation. The medical response to consumer demands for involvement emphasises the unique importance of the patient − provider dyad. Potential benefits of improving this relationship include increased compliance and reduced pressure on professional services for treatment of 'trivial' illness.

Nursing appears to identify itself more closely with the ideal of increased patient autonomy as a desirable end in itself. The nurse's role is to assist the patient towards independence, and to act as his spokesperson where necessary. However, there are tensions in this role and these need to be worked through in theory, practice and research.

2 The active patient

AREA SELECTED FOR REVIEW AND RATIONALE

Chapter 2 examines the active patient concept by:

- constructing, from the literature, a model of the active patient;
- considering the level of activity thought appropriate for different groups of patients;
- reviewing research studies of patient participation preferences;
- looking at ways in which patients can be prepared for participation;
- reviewing studies that have sought to involve patients in aspects of care.

This review is not restricted to nursing literature, but neither is it completely comprehensive. As already indicated, there are gaps in many areas. In other areas there are clusters of very similar studies. Of course, these well-researched topics are the ones about which we can draw the most valid conclusions. Sometimes, however, the conclusions are of limited interest or relevance to nurses, or they serve to divert attention from more important areas. For example, there are numerous studies aimed at improving patient compliance with medication, especially that for hypertension. If health-care professionals believe that regular medication can have long-term benefits for the patient, they are obviously eager for patients to 'keep taking the tablets'. On the other hand, to devote much space to studies of compliance obscures the fact that it is only one, and a rather narrow, interpretation of participation. In any case, the subject has been well reviewed already (e.g. Ross, 1987). This is true also of some other aspects of participation, which will be mentioned but not reviewed in detail. The intention is to provide an overview of research in this area.

METHODOLOGY

Material was selected from the following sources:

1.   Articles, going back to 1983, listed in *Index Medicus* and the *International Nursing Index*, for the subjects 'patient participation', 'consumer participation', 'self-care', 'attitudes to health' and related headings, including 'self-medication', 'patient compliance', 'professional – patient relations', etc.
2.   References contained in articles located from method 1, and from the article 'The Activated Patient: Dogma, Dream, or Desideratum?' by Steele and colleagues (1987). There was no cut-off date for these items.

Review articles were included.

From this body of literature, I have selected elements to illustrate the lines of research being followed. The following sections also contain references to theoretical and descriptive material relevant to an understanding of the research. The limitations of this approach are considered in chapter 4.

A MODEL OF THE ACTIVE PATIENT

Parsons (1951) introduced the concept of the sick role, suggesting that certain privileges were granted to people because they were ill. These include exemption from responsibility for their state of health and exemption from fulfilment of normal social roles. Corresponding obligations include having the motivation to get well, seeking technically competent help, trusting the doctor and compliance with prescribed treatment. Thus, the patient is placed in a passive dependent role. The doctor is granted the privileges of autonomy and professional dominance. He is given licence to define illness and confer the sick status on potential patients. The doctor's obligations are to act with beneficence, to follow the rules of professional conduct (e.g. confidentiality), and to be knowledgeable and expert in his practice.

The sick role concept has been widely criticised (e.g. Freidson, 1961) and modified (e.g. Suchmann, 1965), but most commentators tend to take patient dependency for granted (Haug and Lavin, 1981). Competing models have arisen, as described, emphasising mutuality. So, in place of the passive individual in Parsons' sick role, we have a new, dynamic being: the 'active' or 'activated' patient.

Sehnert and Eisenberg's activated patient (1975) is:

> 'a kind of hearty hybrid who is three-quarters patient and one-quarter physician. They've learned to speak the doctor's own language, and ask him questions rather than passively sit, honour and obey. They've learned to check vital signs, the first signs of a coronary and how to tell whether a sinus problem is an allergy or a common cold by the colour of the mucous membrane of the nose. They've learned Body Talk – that special language of symptoms that enables them to know what an ache or pain is saying. And they are playing an important and needed role in health partnership with the doctors.'

Steele et al (1987) produce a very clear, although slightly more restrained, picture of the active patient, and examine some of the claims made for this model. According to their ideal, active patients reject the passivity of the sick role and assume responsibility for their own care. They:

- ask questions;
- seek explanations;
- state preferences;
- offer opinions;
- expect to be heard.

As a result of this behaviour:

- the dialogue of the medical encounter will expand (Brody, 1980);
- greater interactional symmetry will emerge (Roter, 1977; Greenfield et al, 1985).

This will produce a more complete sharing of information and an expanded knowledge base, and consequently:

- the patient will develop more realistic treatment expectations;
- the provider will be in a position to negotiate individualised, patient-centred treatment plans (Benarde and Mayerson, 1978; Brody, 1980; Quill, 1983);

- higher levels of agreement between professional and patient will be achieved (Starfield et al, 1979, 1981; Speedling and Rose, 1985);
- patients will develop a greater sense of commitment to, and confidence in, the plan of treatment (Schulman, 1979).

Finally, patients will be:

- more satisfied (e.g. Putnam et al, 1985);
- more adherent to treatment (e.g. Schulman, 1979);
- more likely to experience physical, psychological and functional benefits from the treatment provided (e.g. Greenfield et al, 1985).

The following sections look at some of these claims in more detail.

THE SPECTRUM OF PATIENT PARTICIPATION

I have already referred to the work of Szasz and Hollender (1956). At this point it is especially relevant, because it implies the existence of a spectrum, or continuum, of patient participation. (Szasz and Hollender's models apply strictly to the physician – patient interaction, but they are extended here to the interaction of any health-care professional and patient.) The continuum progresses from the passive patient and the active professional ('activity – passivity' model), through the more active patient and less active professional ('guidance – cooperation' model), to the stage where the level of activity of the protagonists approaches equality ('mutual participation'). Here 'the physician does not profess to know exactly what is best for the patient. The search for this becomes the essence of the therapeutic interaction'.

The appropriateness of each level of activity depends on the type of health problem; thus, patient passivity is regarded as normal in very acute illness but as potentially dysfunctional in chronic illness. Szasz and Hollender contend that mutual participation becomes more necessary and appropriate the greater the intellectual, educational and experiential similarities between patient and professional. We may wish to reject this, but there remains a feeling that, irrespective of the type of health problem, some patients have more 'potential' (Lambertson, 1958) for participation than others. Without utilising the inflammatory terminology of class, race, intelligence or educational achievement, it appears difficult to specify criteria for an appropriate level of participation. At least, there is little evidence in the general literature of serious attempts to do so. Instead, the judgment of the individual practitioner tends to be the determining factor. For instance, a district nurse (Jones, 1988) writes of her patient:

> 'She had a very positive attitude and expressed a desire eventually to be free of the district nursing service. It was then that I decided she would be a good patient with whom to try the Orem self-care model of nursing.'

Also, there is evidence that Szasz and Hollender's attitude prevails in practice; it has been noted that doctors provide higher social class patients with more information than those in lower social classes (Waitzkin and Stoeckle, 1972). Attempts have been made to measure the rather different concept of patient *preference* for participation, as reviewed below.

Returning to the spectrum of participation, Freidson (1970a) notes the logical and empirical defects of Szasz and Hollender's scheme, in that it represents a continuum only of the degree to which the *patient* assumes an active role, without being extended to the point where the professional assumes a passive role:

> 'Such a defect reflects the characteristically normative stance of the medical thinker: while the existence of situations where the practitioner more or less does what the patient asks him to do may not be denied, such situations are rejected out of hand as intolerably non-professional, non-therapeutic, and non-dignified.'

Two other patterns of interaction are required, according to Freidson, to complete the continuum: one in which the patient guides and the professional cooperates, and one in which the patient is active and the physician passive. Freidson finds it difficult to imagine an empirical instance of the latter, but this is possibly because his analysis, as for Szasz and Hollender's, is restricted to the doctor – patient interaction in the former's 'office'. Even in this situation, the doctor may play a largely passive role: patients are sometimes prepared, or even expected, to tell their general practitioner (GP) what they want from the visit. However, whether they get it is, in the end, up to the GP, so this interaction conforms more closely to patient-guidance and doctor-cooperation than to true professional passivity. Nurses are seen by patients as more approachable (Oakley, 1984; Stilwell, 1986) and are probably freer to negotiate over the whole of the continuum, although there may be some resistance to the idea of professional passivity and letting the patient 'call the shots'.

I suggest that a further pattern of participation is actually required to complete the continuum: one in which the patient functions alone, without professional support. Of course, logically, this cannot be regarded as a model of *interaction*, but it serves to emphasise the fact that patients (although not so labelled) can manage health problems themselves, and do so to a very great extent (see chapter 5). On the other hand, professionals are dependent on patients to justify their existence. In this sense, it is the professional rather than the patient who 'participates' in health.

In summary, the continuum of patient participation extends from complete passivity to full activity, and the professional's level of activity varies inversely with the patient's. At what point on the continuum an interaction (including care-giving) occurs depends, theoretically, on the type of health problem, the patient's preference and his potential for participation (which remains, for adults, a nebulous concept). However, the professional must also be willing to take up the complementary stance, and such a conceptualisation begs the question of who decides how active the patient is to be. A number of research studies has looked at the process of negotiation and decision-making, as discussed below, but the initiative tends to rest with the professional:

> 'Practising (sic) physicians must frequently make decisions about how much they wish to encourage patient participation in clinical decision-making.' (Brody, 1980)

The concept of a continuum, or spectrum, of participation is usefully descriptive, but it requires development. It tends to focus on only two elements – one patient and one professional. If two professionals are involved (say, the GP and the district nurse) and the patient's family is included, the situation becomes much more complex. Added to this, increased patient activity may require, or call forth, *increased* professional activity, rather than passivity (Martin, 1978). Indeed, this is the very raison d'etre of the consumer movement (Kuhn, 1985).

PATIENT PARTICIPATION PREFERENCES

This section looks at evidence concerning patients' willingness and desire to participate in health care.

Haug and Lavin (1979) conducted a survey of health-centre patients to estimate the extent of public challenge of physician authority. More than half of the sample (n = 640) demonstrated attitudes tending to reject physicians' right to direct their interaction with patients. These attitudes were related to younger age, higher educational level and greater health knowledge. Challenging behaviour (e.g. seeking a second opinion, expressing disagreement with recommendations) occurred at least once for half the group. Respondents' health status, race, sex and pattern of insurance cover had little impact on either attitude or behaviour.

However, Haug and Lavin's model accounted for only 27% of the variance in attitudes and 13% of the variance in challenging behaviours, suggesting that other factors were at work. Questions can also be raised about the way they sought to identify a consumerist stance. For instance, to score at the low end of the attitudinal challenge scale, one would have to endorse attitudes such as 'obedience and respect for what doctors tell you is most important' and 'every person should have complete faith in doctors and do what they tell you without a lot of questions'. The range of behavioural challenges offered, such as changing doctors or actively seeking a second opinion, was rather narrow and extreme, although these options may be more open to North American patients. The terminology of this study is also interesting: even expressing an opinion is interpreted as 'challenging physician authority'. Is this the interpretation of the doctors, the patients or the researchers, one wonders?

Cassileth and associates (1980) explored the degree to which cancer patients preferred to be informed about and to participate in their medical care. The sample (n = 256) completed an Information Styles Questionnaire, designed to elicit data on patient information and participation preference, and the Beck Hopelessness Scale. The attitudes and behaviour of most patients reflected what the authors regard as the contemporary ideal of increased patient participation. The younger the patients, the more they wished to be informed and to participate in decision-making. Older patients, and those more seriously ill, preferred a more non-participatory role. Patients wishing to be involved in treatment decisions were significantly more hopeful than others. The majority of patients in each age group displayed high levels of hope, preference for open communication and a desire for maximum amounts of information.

Cassileth and colleagues tend to play down the sizeable proportion of patients (half those in the 60 and over age group) who indicated a preference for the physician making decisions. There is room for different patient interpretation of questions such as 'I prefer to participate in decisions about my medical care and treatment', and a suspicion that such a response might be seen by patients as socially desirable (although Haug and Lavin regarded preference for physician domination as the socially desirable response). Also, of patients originally approached, 49 (17%) declined or proved ineligible (3 illiterate, 31 too sick or too tired, 4 no time to spare, 11 no specific reason given). Most of these patients could have fallen into the group preferring non-participation. (Perhaps this is a general methodological problem with studies of participation preferences: a self-selected sample will consist of those able and willing to participate. They may be general 'participators' when compared with those not included in the sample.)

Faden et al (1981) surveyed a sample (n = 53) of young, adult, married, white and fairly well-educated out-patients with epilepsy ('seizure disorders'). Questionnaires were designed to elicit what patients wanted to know, and what physicians actually reported disclosing. In general, it was found that patients preferred far more detailed disclosures than doctors routinely offered. Patients preferred extensive disclosure, particularly regarding risks and alternatives to treatment. Doctors only disclosed risks with a relatively high probability of occurrence, and provided little information on alternative treatments. Patients were also more likely to feel that decisions on medication should rest with them. This was a convenience sample and may not be representative of patients with epilepsy. Although there was a strong preference for information, only half the sample expressed a willingness to take final responsibility for deciding treatment.

Strull et al (1984) administered questionnaires on decision-making to 210 hypertensive out-patients and their (50) doctors. They found that 41% of patients wanted more information about hypertension than they had received; doctors underestimated patient preference for discussion about medication in 29% of cases, and overestimated in 11%. Fifty three per cent of patients wished to participate in decisions; doctors believed that patients wished to participate in 78% of cases. The researchers concluded that doctors generally underestimate patients' desire for information and discussion but overestimate patients' desire to make decisions. Younger patients, those with more education, and patients who had been longer in treatment were those most likely to express a preference for active participation.

Strull and colleagues found that out-patients consistently reported receiving more information about hypertension than the doctors reported giving. Fifty two per cent reported that they had received 'quite a lot' of information or 'all there is to know', although doctors reported giving this amount of information in only 38% of cases. This creates the worrying impression that some patients, although not deliberately misled, think that they are in 'full possession of the facts' when this is not the case. However, no account seems to have been taken of information received from other sources. So, although the doctor reported giving less than complete information, it might have been sufficient to complete the patient's knowledge, particularly if these patients asked questions to fill the gaps, which is not recorded. Of 256 consecutive, eligible patients, 46 (16%) did not participate in the study; we are given no details about this group.

Pendleton and House (1984) measured preferences for degree of involvement in health care of 47 low-income, inner-city diabetic out-patients, using the Krantz Health Opinion Survey (Krantz et al, 1980). On comparing these scores with three groups of well college students, significant differences were found, the diabetic patients having lower preference for behavioural involvement and information. Pendleton and House suggest that the difference is related to socioeconomic status (including education), affliction with chronic illness and age. What they interpret as lack of interest in being actively involved is seen as striking in view of the fact that diabetes mellitus requires active, long-term involvement in care.

The authors do not attempt to estimate the level of involvement in their care offered to these patients. Possibly their 'lack of interest' is an adaptive response to the necessity of protracted dealings with a health-care system that does not permit participation, particularly for those of lower socioeconomic status and increased age. Taken too seriously, this might produce something of a Catch 22 situation: patients are not offered participation, so they learn to 'prefer' non-participation; because they seem to prefer non-participation, they are not offered the chance to participate. The designers of the Health Opinion Survey themselves point out that, while this instrument may be useful for assessing generalised orientations to information-seeking and self-care in the management of minor ailments, its utility as a measure of active patient involvement in the management of chronic illness is questionable.

Schulman (1977) developed an Active Patient Orientation (APO) scale and used it to investigate the relationship between varying APO levels and treatment outcomes in hypertensive out-patients (1979). Disappointingly perhaps, APO refers to the orientation of the clinic staff, rather than of the patients; it attempts to measure how much participation was being offered. Few details of the scale are given in the published account (1979). It consists of 11 statements describing the various aspects of APO, for example, 'The staff give me very useful instructions for taking care of my blood pressure'. Patients are asked to respond to each statement by indicating their agreement or disagreement on a four-point scale. However, Schulman's study does have incidental relevance to patient participation preferences because the statements presented to patients seem to confound staff and patient orientation. For instance, irrespective of the actual quality of instruction given, it requires subjective judgment by the patient to decide whether these instructions are 'very useful' or not.

In summary, there seems to be a preference among patients for more information and discussion and, perhaps to a lesser extent, for participation in decision-making. However, there are variations among populations, possibly related to age and socioeconomic status. Preference may be influenced by existing levels of participation. These studies relate almost exclusively to patient – doctor interaction in American primary care settings. The methodologies employed could probably be improved and applied to patient preference for participation in nursing care. Before-and-after studies might be useful to see if a system offering higher levels of participation would call forth a more – or less – enthusiastic response.

PREPARING THE PATIENT FOR PARTICIPATION

This is an important area, and one in which nurses have made very valuable contributions. I shall look briefly at the role of information and information-giving, the concept of informed consent and effective-patient training.

Of course, preparing patients for particpation does not necessarily imply a higher level of patient activity: a patient can be effectively prepared for a passive role, for example in barium enema administration (Wilson-Barnett, 1978), cardiac catheter-isation (Finesilver, 1978) or dental treatment (Auerbach et al, 1983; Winn, 1988). However increased patient activity is often the desired end, for example in preparing patients for self-management of chronic illness. Very occasionally, increased patient participation is seen as the unwanted by-product of obligatory information-giving (Miller, 1974).

The role of information

Brownlea (1987) succinctly states:

'A key requirement for participation is access to the appropriate information base. Participants need to be able to ask questions and get answers and to know that those answers represent the "true" state of the problem being addressed.'

This area has been generally well reviewed: many research studies point to the critical role of information in permitting patients to adapt to the stress of illness, in reducing anxiety and in promoting recovery (e.g. Wilson-Barnett, 1984; Hames and Stirling, 1987). This evidence is supplemented by first-person accounts of life-threatening illness (e.g. Inglefinger, 1980; Clement-Jones, 1985; Mullan, 1985). Patient preference studies, as discussed, generally elicit a preference for full information. When preference for information and decision-making is tested, patients often express a stronger preference for receiving information than for active decision-making.

There has been an historical shift in the amount of information disclosed to patients, especially, perhaps, in the revelation of cancer diagnoses. Whereas most doctors in the 1950s preferred not to reveal the diagnosis of cancer (Oken, 1961), by the late 1970s most physicians told their patients that they had cancer (Novack et al, 1979). The current approach can be seen as deriving from the new emphasis on individual responsibility. Informed consent, open communication, full disclosure, patient teaching and education are expressions of this contemporary focus (Cassileth et al, 1980). Cassileth et al suggest that the strong correlation that they found between preference for maximum information and desire for participation ($p < 0.0001$) indicates that information styles and participation preferences represent components of a single attitude or approach.

However, care is required. Although adequate and appropriate information is required for participation, not all patients wish to participate. Assumptions – for instance, that more information is always better than less – sometimes prove unwarranted when put to the test. In a review of the literature on communication of information to cancer patients, McIntosh (1974) concluded that existing research was inadequate to answer questions as to how, when, how much and what type of information patients should be given. The body of research in this area is growing, although there is still room for development.

Auerbach et al (1976), for instance, found that dental patients with an internal locus of control coped better when given specific preparatory information, while patients with an external locus of control did better when given only general information. Looking at information preference instead of locus of control, Auerbach et al (1983) found that patients scoring high on information preference coped better with surgery when given specific rather than general information. Patients scoring low on information preference adjusted better with general information. In this study they also considered the variable of information-giver hostility and dominance: both low and high information preference groups were split and presented with information in a personalised or relatively impersonal fashion, using non-verbal cues. Patients' perceptions of information-giver hostility were significantly (inversely) related to adjustment.

Fahrenfort (1987) recognises an implicit assumption, made by many authors, that information-flow in itself promotes patient autonomy:

'Being told by the physician the standard medical regimen for your ailment in the assumption that you will go home and follow it, is information. Not very open information, nor very effective in inducing either trust or compliance, but still information.'

D'Onofrio (1980) writes of 'participatory education' as a process in which providers and consumers recognise that they can learn from each other:

'In this way we can all increase our understanding and our options, decide together how best to resolve the problems of medical care, and pool our resources towards these ends.'

Participatory education may provide new power to achieve patient treatment goals, but it should also help to reshape institutions to meet changing needs. This is inspiring rhetoric, but operationalising the concept of participatory education may be difficult.

I have used 'information-giving', 'teaching' and 'education' almost as if they were interchangeable. Given their fullest contemporary meanings, this may not be the case. For instance, Wilson-Barnett and Osborne (1983) distinguish between teaching and information-giving: teaching refers to an interactive process whereby learning takes places that may subsequently be used to influence behaviour. 'Education' is generally seen as a higher order process than teaching. (The word's etymology is often the subject of learned debate: a letter to the Editor of *The Independent* [25 Nov 87] pointed out that Columella used 'educatrix' to mean a nurse.) However, at their best, all three can be interactive processes, sensitively tailored to the needs of the patient.

Informed consent

The first legal mention of 'informed consent' seems to have been in 1914 in relation to surgery (Brody, 1980). It developed as a legal mechanism for extending the liability of physicians in the event of injury to the patient (Kaufmann, 1983). In both Britain and the USA, the laws governing informed consent are those of battery (Dyer and Bloch, 1987). Informed consent was first applied to medical experimentation during the Nuremberg Trials in 1947, and current standards for this area were set out in the Declaration of Helsinki in 1965. Dyer and Bloch state:

'Informed consent is usually considered to be the process whereby explicit communication of information is provided, which would be relevant for a patient or experimental subject to decide whether or not to have a particular treatment or to participate in a particular experiment.'

It has three components; consent must be:

- informed;
- voluntary;
- competent.

Philosophical justification for this doctine is held to rest on the principle of autonomy (Beauchamp and Childress, 1979), and it is, therefore, closely allied to the concept of patient participation. Problems arise in defining what constitutes 'information' for the purposes of consent. As previously discussed in the case of *Sidaway* v. *Bethlem Royal Hospital* (1984), this decision ultimately lies with the doctor. Another difficulty lies in assessing the patient's competence: in extreme cases refusal to consent to treatment may be interpreted as, in itself, evidence of incompetence (Kennedy, 1978). This is probably of greatest significance in the psychiatric setting but, elsewhere, the professional's informal assessment of competence will undoubtedly influence the amount and type of information offered. Although consent must be voluntary, this becomes less meaningful if full information has not been given and discussion of treatment options permitted. The increasing responsibility taken by nurses for information-giving and patient advocacy highlights differing professional interpretations of informed consent (Wilson-Barnett, 1986).

Kaufmann (1983) charts the cumulative growth over the previous two decades in medical, legal and social sciences research literature on patient decision-making and informed consent to medical treatment. The growth curve is sigmoidal and indicates increasing interest among professionals. Supporters of the doctrine have promoted it as a vehicle for establishing patients' rights and a basis for challenging the autonomy of doctors in administering medical care (Demy, 1971; Katz, 1976). Doctors tend to focus on the conflict between the principle of autonomy as a legal concept and the realities of clinical practice that make involvement of patients in medical decisions difficult if not impossible, for example in the emergency situation (Tait and Winslow, 1977). Informed consent has been seen as undermining the fiduciary relationship between the doctor and his patient (Ingelfinger, 1980). The legal requirements for disclosure may be regarded as a sign of bad faith in the doctor's ability to recommend the best treatment, and there is a fear that knowing the risks of the procedure will unduly worry the patient and cause him or her to reject treatment essential for health (Burnham, 1966).

Specifications for informed consent, in the USA, at least, are becoming more detailed. For instance, Weiss (1985) describes legislation in Massachusetts and California requiring patients with breast cancer to be provided with 'complete information on all alternative treatments which are medically viable'. There have been calls for improved access to information for these patients in Britain also (King's Fund, 1986).

In response to such developments, the concept of beneficent paternalism has been rehabilitated. Lomas (1981) suggests that it is not paternalistic empathically to withhold information from patients. Weiss (1985) writes:

> 'The concept of patient autonomy emphasises procedure and the right of patients to decide for themselves, modern paternalism emphasises outcomes and the principles of patient's best interests.'

The modern paternalist's goal is to improve care rather than to provide patient autonomy (an exactly contradictory view to that expressed by Cassell [1976]).

Empirical studies on the comprehension of information for informed consent show that research subjects often do not understand major portions of that to which they have consented (Silva and Sorrell, 1984). Silva and Sorrell review the literature on factors influencing comprehension of information for informed consent: these include the nature of the information, the method of presentation, demographic factors such as age, and personal factors such as reading ability. They conclude that the extent of non-comprehension raises the ethical question of whether or not the consent process has accomplished its purpose – 'the protection of the individual's right to self-determination'. Similarly, Robb (1983) says 'Beware the "Informed" Consent'. She feels that the concept of informed consent is failing in its aims to protect the rights of human subjects in research, particularly in the case of the elderly in long-term care.

Burrows-Hudson (1985) reviewed the literature on assuring informed choice. In one study (McNeil et al, 1982), the researchers looked at the way in which varying the presentation of possible outcomes of different therapies for lung cancer affected patient preference for treatment method. Their results indicated that the risk of perioperative death seemed greater to patients when presented in terms of death than when presented in terms of survival. Burrows-Hudson comments:

> 'Such research provides a valuable lesson in how presentation can affect the patient's decision and it opens up the question of patient and health professional bias with regard to information disclosure and responsiveness.'

The legal requirements for informed consent, in areas other than psychiatry, receive most attention in relation to surgery and research. The patient's right to information is less clear for other forms of treatment (Kingman, 1986).

Summary

In preparation for participation patients require, and generally express a preference for, accurate, relevant and sensitively provided information. Even in situations where passivity is the only option, information is vital for the purposes of consent and, in some cases, to enhance feelings of personal control.

Effctive-patient training

Programmes like those of Sehnert and Eisenberg (1975) and Pratt (1971) start with well clients. As will be discussed in the final section of this account, this may be the most effective place to begin. Here mention will be made only of interventions with patients, as previously defined.

Roter (1977) equates patient autonomy with question-asking, because professionals tend to see this behaviour as an expression of the patient's desire to be actively involved. Question-asking creates a 'bilateral' situation by requiring some sort of response. On this basis, Roter developed a patient education programme to encourage question-asking. Hypertensive patients (n = 294) were randomly allocated to a control ('placebo') group, given only general information about the clinic before their doctor's appointment, or to an experimental group in which a health educator helped them to identify and rehearse questions about their condition and its treatment. The subsequent doctor – patient interactions were audiotape-recorded and patients completed a questionnaire to assess their satisfaction and locus of control.

Patient question-asking increased from 1.21 questions per

encounter in the control group to 2.12 questions in the experimental group. However, 'activated' patient encounters displayed more tension, anxiety and anger on the part of the patients than did those of the control group. The experimental group were also less satisfied with their visits, but they displayed better appointment-keeping over a four-month follow-up period. Experimental group patients scored higher on internal locus of control. Roter concludes that patient education increased information-seeking and improved communication skills. This created an implicit challenge to the passive patient role and led to anxiety, contributing to the negative affective trend of the interaction. The sense of dissonance between their expected passivity and the activity of question-asking caused the patients to alter their 'self-views', as reflected in higher internal locus of control. This change manifested itself in improved appointment-keeping.

Outcome measures, other than appointment-keeping, are missing from this study, and the follow-up period was rather short. The only unequivocal result is that patients can be activated to ask more questions. This is a potentially fruitful line of approach for nurses, but the implications of increasing patient anxiety, particularly in hypertensive patients, need to be seriously considered. Also, care is required to prevent subversion of the therapeutic alliance between doctor and patient. Perhaps it is not surprising that preparing patients for an 'encounter' with a doctor creates anxiety.

Along similar lines, Greenfield et al (1985) developed an intervention to inform out-patients being treated for peptic ulcers about the medical care process and to improve their information-seeking, enabling them to interact more effectively with their doctors. In a 20-minute session immediately preceding a scheduled appointment a trained clinic assistant reviewed the previous visit with the patients showing them their medical record. The patients were helped to identify relevant medical decisions made about their care and management issues warranting discussion with the doctor.

Experimental group patients (n = 23) were encouraged to ask questions, recognise the need for a decision on management and negotiate these decisions with the doctor. A control group (n = 22) were given general information about ulcer disease and treatment; they were not shown their medical records nor encouraged to identify problems.

Audiotape-recordings of the doctor – patient interaction showed that patients in the experimental group were twice as effective as control group patients in obtaining information from doctors. Six to eight weeks after the trial, patients in the experimental group reported fewer limitations in physical and role-related activities, stated that they preferred their more active role in decision-making, and were as satisfied as the control group with their care.

The affective component of the doctor – patient interaction received little attention in this study. The experimental group spoke more, and more rapidly, than did the control group, but the researchers report that the audiotapes did not show any increase in patient tension during consultations. Experimental group patients did not ask significantly more questions; they seemed to adopt alternative strategies in order to obtain information, such as joking about their uncertainties and introducing concerns attributed to others. This shows considerable subtlety on the part of patients, and the strategies were effective in eliciting information. The intervention was supposedly designed in such a way as to stress the non-adversarial nature of patient involvement, but the possibility also exists that the doctors were more receptive to patient involvement than were those in Roter's study.

More sophisticated outcome measures would be a useful development for such studies. In the latter case, improvements in health status were estimated only subjectively by patients. Most studies aimed at promoting participation deal with conditions such as hypertension and diabetes, partly because physiological outcomes can be measured more readily. The mechanism by which increased involvement in care leads to improved health outcomes requires further step-by-step elucidation.

ASPECTS OF PARTICIPATION

It was my original intention to sort these studies into stages of the nursing process, that is, those dealing with assessment, planning, implementation and evaluation of care. In fact, I have arranged them differently for two main reasons:

1.   It proved difficult to disentangle the various stages. Many
      studies are conducted in out-patient settings and concentrate

on doctor – patient interaction. Patients tend to present with a fairly narrow range of problems, expecting immediate treatment or advice. Assessment and planning are less demarcated in this case. On the other hand, studies relating to goal-setting often conceptualise this process as part of both planning and intervention (Hill and Smith, 1985).

2. Limitations on time and space have caused me to restrict the variety of studies reviewed. To some extent, I have chosen to reflect the 'prejudices' of the literature; the following themes are among those most prevalent.

The negotiated approach to patienthood

A series of studies by Lazare, Eisenthal and their colleagues in the out-patient psychiatric setting sought to encourage health-care professionals to adopt a 'customer approach' to patienthood. Patients are assumed to have knowledge and opinions about their problems and to present with certain expectations about how the therapist can, or should, help. Lazare et al's customer approach stresses:

- the eliciting and understanding of the requests that patients have regarding how they hope to be helped;
- the negotiating of a treatment plan with the patients.

One study (Eisenthal and Lazare, 1976) attempted to evaluate this approach from the patient's perspective. Sixteen staff in a 'walk-in' psychiatric clinic received lectures on the customer approach, that is, training in how to elicit information and preferences from patients. They remained unaware of the purpose of the study. Patients (n = 106) were asked to complete a questionnaire, after their initial interview, designed to assess how customer-oriented the therapist was, how satisfied and helped patients felt and their perception of symptom change.

Patients perceiving the therapist to be using the customer approach had substantially improved outcomes, especially in terms of feeling satisfied and helped. This held even when patients did not receive the treatment they had initially envisaged. Among four index items for customer approach, the two most highly correlated with feeling satisfied and helped were the clinician helping the patient to put his request into words, and the patient participating in the treatment planning.

A second study (Eisenthal et al, 1979) investigated the relationship between the negotiated approach and adherence. (Eisenthal suggests that the term 'adherence', rather than compliance, conveys the preferred implication of choice and mutuality in treatment planning.) In a similar setting to the previous study, questionnaires to assess the therapist's customer-orientation were administered to 130 patients. Information on adherence was obtained from the patients' records, although adherence was judged only in terms of attendance at the referral appointment after the initial clinic assessment. Adherence was found to be significantly related to the patient getting the treatment plan he wanted.

Eisenthal et al (1983) examined the relationship between patient and doctor satisfaction and the negotiated approach to the initial psychiatric interview in a third study. Two dimensions of the negotiated approach were distinguished:

- mutuality in communicating explanatory information;
- mutuality in making treatment decisions.

Transcripts (n = 44) of patients' interviews with therapists were independently rated on each of 10 negotiated-approach process measures, five measures of explanatory communication and five of participation. At the conclusion of the interview, three kinds of satisfaction rating were obtained: the patient's satisfaction, the therapist's perception of patient satisfaction and the therapist's own satisfaction.

Patient satisfaction was associated with:

- *explanatory processes:* being given clear and complete explanations concerning the recommended treatment plan, its rationale and its link to the patient's complaint;
- *decision-making processes:* stating a request and reaching a consensus with the therapist on the treatment plan.

Negotiation was not significantly correlated with therapist satisfaction and therapists were inaccurate in their perception of the sources of patient satisfaction.

Most of the correlations found by Eisenthal and associates were modest. Overall, the relationship between satisfaction and information-giving was more significant than that between satisfaction and decision-making. There are problems in operationalising the concept of shared decision-making. Patients were encouraged to express their requests, and discussion occurred, but it is difficult to track down to what extent patients' views contributed to the final treatment decision.

Starfield et al (1979) studied patient – doctor agreement about problems needing a follow-up visit. The sample consisted of patients visiting an urban group practice during a 2-month period who were given a follow-up appointment within the next 3 months (n = 215). At the conclusion of their initial (index) visit, patients and providers were interviewed to determine:

- the items they thought required follow-up on the next visit;
- the extent to which they anticipated each problem would be improved by then.

At the conclusion of the second visit patients were interviewed to determine:

- the degree of improvement of each item listed at the initial visit;
- whether there were any unanswered questions about these items;
- the overall satisfaction with the current visit.

The patient's medical record was examined for evidence that problems noted at the index visit were recognised by the doctor at the second visit.

Patients and practitioners agreed on the need for follow-up for only 45% of the problems mentioned by either after the initial visit. Problems mentioned by both doctor and patient were much more likely to be discussed at follow-up than were problems mentioned only by one participant, and patients reported more improvement with the former group of problems. It may be that patient problems not listed by doctors are not dealt with to the extent that other problems are, and that patients expect a poorer outcome. On the other hand, problems not mentioned by doctors may be less amenable to therapy and may not be discussed for this reason. However, the authors suggest that these problems should at least receive acknowledgement, so that patients do not have unrealistic expectations. The listing of important problems by the patient and the doctor would require little extra time and might lead to improved recognition of patients' problems and better outcomes of care.

A second study by Starfield et al (1981), of similar design, supported the findings of the previous study that practitioner – patient agreement about problems is associated with greater expectations for improvement and with better outcome as perceived by patients. In this study, doctors also reported better outcomes of care for problems listed by both.

Goal-setting

Goals are sometimes seen as distinct from objectives. For instance, goals may be defined as broad statements of intent or outcome, which do not describe the process necessary to reach the goal (e.g. 'I will feel better'), whereas objectives can be quantified and measured (e.g. I will be able to walk 200 yards in one minute') (Bailey and Claus, 1975). Alternatively, 'goal' can be used for specific client or patient aims, because the term is a familiar one, whereas professionals have longer-term, higher-level 'objectives' (Hill and Smith, 1985). I am not sure that this distinction is helpful. What is certain is that nurses need to develop appropriate, detailed treatment goals and help patients to achieve them. Research has moved some distance in this direction. In summary:

> 'findings suggest that the innovation of mutual goal-setting will lead to more effective goal attainment and greater patient satisfaction.' (Conduct and Utilization of Research in Nursing Project, 1982)

The literature on various forms of goal-setting is extensive and could form the subject of an entire review. Much of the evidence relates to health risk reduction with clients (e.g. Alexy, 1985). Only studies with patients will be discussed here.

Hefferin (1979) conducted a study with medical, surgical and psychiatric in-patients, which the Conduct and Utilization of Research in Nursing (CURN) project used as the primary research base for their clinical protocol on mutual goal-setting. In this study, 604 patients and 137 nurses were surveyed to assess their levels of satisfaction with health care. Nurses were also asked for their perception of patient satisfaction. This information served as a baseline. Fifty volunteer nurses were then trained in mutual goal-setting as follows:

- learning to identify patient health goals;
- practice in developing goal-planning statements;
- practice in evaluating patient goal progress;
- use of study instruments.

On completion of this training, 572 new patients were assigned to either experimental or control groups. Experimental group patients were assisted by the trained nurses in mutual goal-setting. Patients in the control group did not participate in goal-setting; nurses set goals for them on the basis of admission assessments. Progress was evaluated at weekly intervals, or on return out-patients visits. Satisfaction levels were recorded for both groups and were compared with the baseline group.

Levels of satisfaction were significantly higher for the experimental group when compared with the baseline and control groups. Nurses perceived the same increase in satisfaction for the experimental group and also estimated a higher level of satisfaction for the controls over the baseline group. Nurse satisfaction was higher for the experimental group patients than for the control or baseline groups, and was in fact, higher for baseline patients than for controls. Hefferin suggests that:

'the project training program may have provided the nurses with a new (or renewed) perspective on the broader care responsibilities and possible satisfactions inherent to the nurse role.'

Patients who participated in developing written goal-planning statements with their nurses made greater progress than did control patients who did not develop such statements. However, it is difficult to know to which aspect of the procedure this improvement is attributable. In other words, if patients participate in setting goals, are the goals selected more appropriate, are patients more motivated to achieve them, are nurses more motivated to assist patients in achieving them, or does the result depend on all three factors? No information is provided on follow-up.

The CURN Project document also discusses a number of other goal-setting studies, in the mental health field, using the method of Goal Attainment Scaling. This is an aid for establishing mutual goals and an evaluation tool for measuring patient progress. Although evidence seems to confirm its reliability and validity, it appears too complex a method for general application and will not be described here. It may be, however, that Goal Attainment Scaling would repay detailed study if this resulted in development of a form more suitable for everyday practice.

Locke et al (1981) reviewed evidence for the influence of goal-setting on performance of a wide range of tasks. They conclude:

'Goals effect performance by directing attention, mobilising effort, increasing persistence and motivating strategy development. Goal setting is most likely to improve task performance when the goals are specific and sufficiently challenging, the subjects have sufficient ability ..., feedback is provided to show progress in relation to the goal, rewards such as money are given for goal attainment, the experimenter or manager is supportive, and assigned goals are accepted by the individual.'

Contingency contracting

Contingency contracting can be seen as a specialised form of goal-setting. The fundamental behavioural principle on which this strategy is based is that individuals tend to behave in ways that lead to outcomes they value, and this behavioural change is likely to be enhanced if incentives are provided to reinforce the desired behaviour (Cameron and Best, 1987). There have been several detailed reviews of contingency contracting, generally related to health education rather than to the identified health problems of patients.

Janz et al (1984), reviewing contingency contracting to enhance consumer compliance, define such a contract as:

'a specific negotiated agreement that provides for the delivery of positive consequences or reinforcers contingent upon desirable behaviour (and sometimes the delivery of negative consequences when undesirable behaviors are displayed).'

Lewis and Michnich (1977) stress the aspect of *mutual* responsibility in their definition:

'negotiated agreements between the parties as to the relative and absolute authority and responsibility of each in achieving a defined goal or objective that is mutually decided upon by both.'

Such a definition, however, does not seem to distinguish contingency contracting from other forms of goal-setting, as mentioned above.

The contract usually involves the patient in the therapeutic decision-making process, and capitalises upon the patient – provider relationship thereby created. Additional incentives ('reinforcers') are provided for treatment objectives. Clarifying the relative responsibilities of both provider and consumer through the explicit exchange of information, as Lewis and Michnich envisage, creates a real, or perceived, transfer of power from the provider to the patient.

However, Janz et al note that the relative contribution to outcome made by the various aspects of contracting has not been explored. For example, reported successes may be more a function of the process of forming a contract (that is, formulating definite goals, time-scale, etc.) than of the written contract itself. These authors produce a useful comparative table of the process and outcome variables of 15 studies of contingency contracting, in the areas of weight change, alcoholism, drug abuse, renal disease regimen and hypertensive regimen. They conclude that at least short-term positive effects are obtained from contingency contracting across the range of conditions reviewed. Investigators have reported that contracts are simple to implement and do not add much time to patient – provider interaction.

Various problems in design and methodology limit the validity of results. Recidivism is significant in the few studies that conducted long-term follow up. Generalisability is also questionable, as most studies were conducted with motivated volunteers. Substantial numbers of potential subjects declined to participate after study requirements were described. Further research is required to determine:

- the types of patient for which this strategy is most appealing and effective;
- the skills that providers must acquire to implement contingency contracting;
- the mechanisms for continued contracting or for weaning the patient from contingency dependence;
- the circumstances under which long-term results might be obtained;
- the effectiveness of contracting when used in conjunction with other forms of participation;
- suitable reinforcements, given that it may be unethical to expect (or allow) patients to relinquish money and valuables. (But NHS fund-raisers please note!)

Janz et al suggest that the best type of contract is a 'self-contract', in which the patient administers his or her own reward and the professional is available only for support and advice. This would help to move the patient away from the dependence created by the initial provider – patient contract. Hill and Smith (1985) discuss the process of self-contracting in detail. They define a self-contract as:

'an agreement that an individual makes with himself or herself, with
or without the assistance of a support person. It is used to improve
self-care behavior.'

Self-contracting forms a large component of their 'self-care' approach
to nursing. However, although the ideological and theoretical basis
for this is described, no research is produced to demonstrate the
effectiveness of self-contracting in improving long-term outcomes.

Other areas worthy of review

I have chosen to finish my review at this point. The few aspects of
the active patient model already discussed are those to which most
importance is attached by commentators, such as Steele et al (1987)
and many of the researchers mentioned above. The areas reviewed
focus on preparing patients for, and involving them in, decision-
making, and on patient preference for such involvement. Insofar
as the concept of patient autonomy is principally concerned with
decision-making and control, such emphasis seems justified.

There are, of course, further aspects of patient participation of
which the research evidence merits review. Two such areas,
which have already received considerable critical attention, are
those of self-monitoring (e.g. Nelson, 1977; Cameron and Best,
1987) and self-medication (e.g. Dunnell and Cartwright, 1972;
Ross, 1987). Although there is a significant degree of overlap with
patient participation, research in these areas is perhaps slightly
less relevant to the active patient model than is that reviewed here.
Self-medication may be an alternative course of action to seeking
professional care (that is, to becoming a patient). When patients
are involved, much research concentrates on the issue of
compliance, as observed. Self-monitoring, while undeniably
requiring patient activity, is often presented as a necessity rather
than an option for patients, and is also discussed in terms of
compliance (e.g. Cameron and Best, 1987).

Studies involving patients in the evaluation of care are of
relevance to this account. However, from considerations of time
and space, readers are referred to the interesting reviews by
Locker and Dunt (1978) and Speedling and Rose (1985) and the
recent experimental work of Like and Zyzanski (1987), which all
examine patient satisfaction.

In essence, there is widespread acknowledgement that patients should be involved in evaluation of care (Rovers, 1986). Measures of satisfaction do involve the patient, but there are serious theoretical and methodological difficulties inherent in this approach. In particular, as Speedling and Rose argue, prevailing conceptualisations of patient satisfaction fail to incorporate measures of patient participation in the therapeutic process: satisfaction is generally operationalised solely as a reaction to the medical encounter. While few would argue the desirability of achieving high levels of patient satisfaction, its meaning and significance remain somewhat enigmatic. Difficulties with this concept illustrate the need for new, participatory methods of evaluation.

Finally, the advantages of participation in the various stages of the process of care may complement one other. As Brownlea (1987) writes:

'Clearly, one implication of increased knowledge and shared decision-making . . . is the critical capacity to evaluate the effectiveness of the health care professional.'

Implications for practice and suggestions for further research, together with the limitations of this review, are considered in chapter 4.

3 | Chronic illness

AREA SELECTED FOR REVIEW AND RATIONALE

Having examined the active patient concept in chapter 2, I shall now scrutinise a body of nursing research for evidence of this model in practice. There are two main reasons for proceeding in this way:

- Very few nursing studies on the more active aspects of patient participation (i.e. not on patient teaching or information-giving) were located by the usual means, that is under the headings 'consumer participation', 'patient participation', 'attitudes to health', 'self-care', 'decision-making', etc. in *Index Medicus* and the *International Nursing Index*. This led me to suspect that either the indexing procedure or my search technique was at fault.
- I thought it possible that examination of a discrete body of nursing research literature not specifically related to participation might provide new perspectives or uncover instances of embryonic trends towards participation not sufficiently developed to be indexed as such.

The area for review concerns the community nursing of adult patients with chronic conditions. Many authors regard patient participation as a vital element in the management of chronic illness (e.g. Martin, 1978; Pendleton and House, 1984). Szasz and Hollender (1956) see their model of mutual participation as 'realistic and necessary' for these patients:

'Here the patient's own experiences provide reliable and important clues to therapy. Moreover, the treatment program itself is principally carried out by the patient. Essentially, the physician helps the patient to help himself.'

61

Orienting services to patients as passive recipients of care is probably dysfunctional in the treatment of such diseases (Schulman, 1979). The management of chronic illness is influenced by a number of shared characteristics (Connelly, 1987):

- the illness is long-term in nature, requiring extended if not life-long treatment;
- cure is rarely, if ever, possible;
- treatment tends to be complex and multi-dimensional; recommendations often include taking medication, following special diets, exercise regimes, monitoring and assessing the condition, etc.;
- changes in life-style and habits may be beneficial;
- chronic conditions tend to be managed in the community;
- where possible, patients continue their usual social roles and responsibilities.

These characteristics make participation or self-care potentially valuable:

- *logistically:* professional supervision may be available only sporadically;
- *economically:* the growing number and proportion of the population affected by chronic conditions, their long-term nature and the complexity of treatment make (apparently) cheaper, or more cost-effective, options appealing.
- *therapeutically:* management aims to enhance well-being, avoid risk-factors and prevent complications. Participation is thought to assist achievement of these aims, as discussed below.

Nurses have a major role to play in the management of chronic illness, particularly in the community (VanDam and Bauwens, 1981). The role of the nurse working with chronically ill patients has been described as less that of a provider of direct treatment and more that of a facilitator and supporter of effective self-care behaviours (Connelly, 1987). In one sense, the roles of patient and nurse are reversed in the community, since the patient is 'host' and the nurse a 'guest' (Baly et al, 1987). The fact that the patient is on his own territory emphasises his right to participate in care. Also, according to Pollock (1987), the contribution of nursing research in this area has been substantial. Therefore, if nurses are promoting patient participation at all, research related to chronic illness management in the community should be one of the most fruitful areas in which to find evidence of this.

METHODOLOGY

Articles were selected from six nursing research journals:

1. *Advances in Nursing Science;*
2. *International Journal of Nursing Studies;*
3. *Journal of Advanced Nursing;*
4. *Nursing Research;*
5. *Research in Nursing and Health;*
6. *Western Journal of Nursing Research.*

In addition, articles were taken from *Patient Education and Counseling* if at least one of the authors could be clearly identified as a nurse or as working within a department of nursing. These journals were chosen because they focus on nursing research and theory, contain research on a range of clinical, situational and developmental areas and are refereed (Ganong, 1987). All issues for the 5-year period 1983–1987 were examined.

To be selected for review, articles had to involve some aspect of chronic physical illness in adults, managed largely in the community. Chronic illness was interpreted to include patients with:

- arthritis (osteo- and rheumatoid arthritis);
- diabetes (mellitus types I and II and insipidus);
- hypertension (diagnosed and treated);
- chronic respiratory disease;
- other chronic conditions, such as renal disease and chronic heart failure (excluding recent history of myocardial infarction).

Reluctantly, cancer was excluded, although these articles formed the largest single group. The main reasons for exclusion were the potential diversity of types, symptoms and stages of the disease and the existence of specialised support services, which could make conclusions less generalisable to other chronic conditions. This area related to patient participation could form the subject of a separate review.

Articles dealing with more than one chronic condition were

included, as were theoretical, descriptive and review articles. Articles with ambiguous titles were scanned before a decision was made on their inclusion. In total, 36 articles were located, distributed as follows:

- arthritis   5
- diabetes   7
- hypertension   9
- respiratory disease   7
- other or multiple chronic conditions   8

These articles are briefly reviewed below, in chronological order under disease group. Emphasis is given to aspects potentially relevant to patient participation, either explicit or implicit in the article. This judgment is subjective, based on my original definition of participation (Brownlea, 1987):

> 'Participation means getting involved or being allowed to become involved in a decision-making process or the delivery of a service or the evaluation of a service, or even simply to become one of a number of people consulted on an issue or a matter.'

ARTHRITIS

Lowery et al (1983) conducted an exploratory survey of the causal thinking of arthritics, based on attribution theory, which is concerned with how an individual ascribes a cause to an effect. According to the theory, such causal explanations predict people's behavioural and emotional reaction to life events. Many studies in other fields, particularly in educational settings, have explored the reasons that individuals give for success and failure and the behavioural and affective consequences of such beliefs. From these studies, it has been found that the causes that people give in achievement situations fall along three dimensions:

- *locus*: whether the cause is internal or external to the person;
- *stability*: whether or not the cause is changeable;
- *control*: whether or not the cause is under volitional control or is controlled by outside forces.

The sample for this study consisted of 55 male rheumatoid arthritics. All attenders at an out-patients clinic over a 7-month period were asked to participate; the response rate is not given.

Consenting patients were interviewed by trained nurses and asked to complete the Multiple Affect Adjective Checklist (MAACL), to measure anxiety, depression and hostility, the Convery Index, which measures functional capacity through assessment of daily living skills and mobility, and an Attributions Interview Schedule designed by the investigators. The latter explores the causes ascribed by patients to their disease and their rating of treatment success or failure. A panel of judges scored the causal replies on the three dimensions given above.

Using the scored causal dimensions as predictors, bivariate regression analysis indicated that the three dimensions, taken separately, did not predict the outcome measures of functional capacity, affect and current or future estimates of treatment success. The three dimensions could not be combined as explanatory variables, owing to the limited sample size and clustering of data. Eight patients (15%) had not constructed causes to explain their arthritis. The causes given by the remaining subjects tended to cluster within only a few dimensions, with external, stable and uncontrollable causes (e.g. 'old age coming up', 'the Lord's will') being most often ascribed. Those patients not giving causes were significantly more anxious, depressed and hostile than those giving causes. Results are seen as calling into question the utility of attribution theory in clinical settings and the efficacy of feelings of personal control. Arthritics did not appear to be functioning better when their ascriptions were on the internal, controllable side of the causal scale. The researchers noted that feelings of personal control may not be adaptive if the situation faced is uncertain and uncontrollable in many respects.

Burckhardt (1985) explored the impact of pain and functional impairment on the quality of life (QOL) experienced by people with arthritis. A causal model was developed, based on a cognitive framework in which disease-related variables, interacting with demographic and social factors, were hypothesised to affect QOL through psychological mediation. Their convenience sample consisted of 94 adults (74 women, 20 men) with a variety of chronic arthritic conditions (rheumatoid arthritis 52, osteoarthritis 21, systemic lupus erythematosus 6, ankylosing spondylitis 6 and other forms 8). Data were collected by interview using a semi-structured questionnaire. Instruments included indices to measure QOL, severity of pain and socioeconomic status. The investigator developed indicators for social network configuration, perceived support, severity of impairment and negative attitude towards illness. Internal control over health was measured by the internal locus of control sub-scale of the Multidimensional Health Locus of Control Scales developed by Wallston et al (1978). Path analysis explored the complex relationships suggested by the model, using stepwise multiple regression analysis to derive the path coefficients.

Self-esteem accounted for 25% of the observed variance in QOL. Subjects who were able to maintain a belief in themselves as intelligent, efficient and friendly rated their QOL as highly satisfactory. It was not possible to assess to what extent lack of self-esteem pre-dated the illness or whether the chronic illness led to a loss of self-esteem. Internal locus of health control contributed 20% to explained variance in QOL. Subjects who believed strongly that control over their health was their responsibility, who attributed physical health to taking good care of themselves, and who believed that they had the power to make themselves well had higher scores. The sense of personal control was less marked in subjects with higher impairment. Negative attitude towards the illness accounted for 15% of the explained variance in QOL. Patients who were worried, angry, depressed, discouraged and frustrated about their disease experienced lower QOL ratings. Age and severity of pain contributed to this result. Interestingly, older subjects were less negative about their disease. Ten per cent of explained variance was accounted for by perceived support. Higher QOL scores were experienced by those with several people on whom they could rely for support.

Of the environmental variables, severity of impairment was the only one to show a significant total effect on QOL, contributing 25% to the explained variance, primarily through the mediating variables of self-esteem and internal locus of control. Sex and socioeconomic status contributed little to explaining QOL, but this was probably connected with the marked homogeneity of the sample with respect to these variables (most of the subjects were middle-class, well-educated women). This limits the generalisability of results. Several types of arthritis were represented but, because of the small number in each group, analysis to disentangle the effects of different disease type was not possible.

The researchers concluded that self-esteem, a sense of personal control and supportive relationships play a major role in determining the perception of QOL in persons with arthritis. Pain and functional impairment in this study were mediated through psychological variables. Nursing interventions to reduce pain and impairment should be tested for their effects on these variables and on QOL.

Laborde and Powers (1985) also studied QOL in patients with arthritis. The sample consisted of 160 patients with osteoarthritis from four settings. Subjects completed measures of health locus of control, past, present and anticipated future life satisfaction and perceived health status. Results indicated that although patients rated their usual pain as distressing, their degree of pain did not impinge on their overall QOL. Most subjects rated their QOL as good, although some viewed their past life as more satisfactory than their present. However, as the majority of subjects were retired, loss of employment, rather than disease state or the ageing process, might have affected present life satisfaction. Subjects tended to be externally oriented to health control. It cannot be assumed from this that patients believe health maintenance practices to be beyond their control. Rather, it may be a more realistic orientation, influenced by previous life experiences and acceptance of what the future holds.

Byers (1985) studied the effect of exercise on morning stiffness and mobility in 30 patients with rheumatoid arthritis. Elastic stiffness (measured orthographically) and subjective ratings of stiffness were less, and mobility (measured by goniometer) greater, the morning after evening exercises were performed. In promoting maximum mobility for arthritic patients, nurses need to be aware that appropriate timing of interventions may enhance their effects. This seems to be the case for exercise and may be true for other measures, such as pain relief.

Oermann et al (1986) conducted a control-group pre- and post-test study on 30 rheumatoid arthritic out-patients. The study was designed to measure the effectiveness of a self-instruction programme in terms of knowledge gain, patient satisfaction and health status. One-way analysis of covariance on post-test Rheumatoid Arthritis Knowledge Inventory (RAKI) scores, with the pre-test as covariate, was used to examine the difference in learning between the two groups. The difference was significant ($p = 0.01$): the experimental group had higher post-test scores than the control group. Subjects were satisfied with the teaching approach, as measured on a Likert-type scale developed by the researchers. They rated self-instruction as an effective teaching strategy in terms of learning and acceptability. No significant difference was demonstrated between the groups in health status on the Arthritis Impact Measurement Scales (AIMS), designed to assess physical, emotional and social well-being.

These results must be interpreted with caution for a number of reasons. For example, prior to any teaching, the self-instruction group began the study with significantly higher knowledge scores. The main effect was still found to be significant, but the pre-test scores accounted for most of the difference between groups. Also, educational level was positively correlated with test scores, and the experimental group had higher educational levels than did the control group. It might have been better to evaluate the patient's use of information given, rather than to expect this to be reflected in health status, which is affected by disease state. In spite of the study's shortcomings, the authors regard self-instruction as a potentially valuable strategy, as it provides a means of individualising the teaching, allows the person to progress at his or her own rate and may be more cost-effective than one-to-one teaching.

DIABETES

Given et al (1983) review scales designed to measure health belief constructs, on the basis that 'effective control of diabetes depends in large measure upon patient participation in the disease management'. With a sample of 156 diabetic patients, factor analysis was used to develop measures of the basic concepts of Becker's Health Belief Model (1974), modified to explain the health behaviours of patients with chronic disease. According to this model, participation by patients in the management of their disease is associated with three classes of beliefs:

- conviction of the severity of the disease;
- belief in the efficacy of prescribed therapy;
- belief that barriers to the successful execution of therapeutic behaviours can be surmounted.

Scales to measure these concepts, derived from the first sample, were cross-validated on a second sample of 92 diabetic patients. The scales were tested for unidimensionality and internal and external consistency, but not for validity. The authors discuss the application of these scales to nursing research and practice. They are seen as potentially useful tools for transferring greater responsibility to patients for management of their diabetes. This process should begin with an assessment of patients' beliefs about such issues as their ability to control the effects of diabetes, the barriers to their carrying out therapy and their beliefs regarding that therapy. When nurses understand patients' beliefs they can begin to interact with patients to devise strategies that can alter beliefs and behaviours. The scales can be incorporated into the overall intervention as pre- and post-measures to determine the efficacy of behavioural approaches for increasing patients' responsibility.

O'Connell et al (1984) studied symptomatology in non-insulin-dependent (NID, type II) diabetic patients. Of the 38 patients interviewed, 32 used symptoms as signals of their blood glucose levels and adjusted their diabetes-related actions (e.g. eating or drinking) on this basis. The tendency to take such action was positively related to long-term control of blood glucose as measured by glycosylated haemoglobin. Although health-care providers may minimise the importance of symptoms, patients do not. Objective measures of physiological status have their place, but an understanding of patients' symptom experience is crucial to the promotion of self-care. The authors suggest that their model of self-regulation through symptom control has the potential to explain adherence and non-adherence behaviours in type II diabetic patients and can serve as a useful guide in planning intervention to increase adherence behaviours. Patients experiencing symptoms not relieved by habitual methods may be particularly open to adopting new, more effective methods for controlling them.

Graham and Schubert (1985) designed a patient education programme for patients with diabetes insipidus. Teaching these patients skills in self-observation, diagnostic testing and treatment not requiring medical supervision is regarded as a means of promoting patient independence in self-care. Before the programme was designed nurses interviewed 15 patients, asking them what they knew about the disease and what they wished to know. Results indicated that patients wanted more information about aetiology, symptomatology and their role in the treatment programme. The overall objectives of the teaching plan were for the patient to be able to:

- define central and nephrogenic diabetes insipidus;
- describe his or her role in the treatment of diabetes insipidus;
- differentiate between diabetes insipidus and diabetes mellitus.

The programme involved a videotape, shown over closed circuit television, and an accompanying booklet. All patients interviewed after the programme (number undisclosed) reported that the script met their educational needs about diabetes insipidus. No follow-up or outcome measures are reported.

Jenny (1986) studied differences in adaptation to diabetes between insulin-dependent (ID) and NID patients and the implications for health education. The most common indicator of learning needs is generally seen as the type of disease with which the patient must cope. However, as shown by Jenny's self-report survey of IDDs (n = 138) and NIDDs (n = 108), variations in the expression of disease between individuals often make the problem of adaptation quite different. The IDD group were younger, had longer disease duration, poorer diabetic control and more instruction, and were more compliant with their regime. IDD subjects perceived greater benefit from all aspects of self-care, except for diet and exercise, than did the NIDD subjects. IDD subjects also showed increased concerns and more social support.

The findings are thought to lend moderate support to the idea that increased severity of diabetes is a valid indicator of increased adaptive demand and that patients might benefit from separate teaching sessions, recognising differences in age and disease severity. The generalisability of these findings is limited by the unknown validity and reliability of the self-report questionnaire and the use of a convenience sample. No effort is made to separate the influence of different variables; for instance, it is not known whether age or type of disease is the most significant factor affecting adaptation.

McBride (1987) examined the reliability and construct validity of Kearney and Fleischer's Exercise of Self-Care Agency Scale (1979). The development of the scale was based on Orem's assertion (1985) that unless self-care agency is accurately diagnosed, nurses have no rational basis for making judgments about self-care deficits. According to Orem, self-care agency varies with health state, life experience and factors that influence educability. This instrument had been previously tested for reliability and validity using nursing and psychology students, i.e. healthy young adults. McBride compared two convenience samples of nursing students (n = 52) and adult patients from an out-patient diabetic clinic (n = 57). Guglielmino's Self-Directed Learning Readiness Scale (1978) was used to test construct validity. The results showed significant correlations between scales for both groups, although the relationship was stronger for the student group (*r* = 0.505) than for the patient group (*r* = 0.302). Split-half reliability of the scale under test was similar for both groups (*r* = 0.78 and 0.74) but test – retest reliability was lower for the patient group (*r* = 0.55) than for the students (*r* = 0.76). Results indicate that construct validity needs further attention.

The remaining studies in this group looked at:

- maternal anxiety and sensitive mothering behaviours in diabetic and non-diabetic women (Schroeder-Zwelling and Hock, 1986);
- the outcome of multiple usage of disposable syringes in the insulin-requiring diabetic (Poteet et al, 1987).

HYPERTENSION

The main focus of studies on hypertension appeared to be either the Health Belief Model and its effects on compliance, or factors predictive of good hypertensive control.

DeVon and Powers (1984) compared health beliefs influencing compliance, and psychosocial adjustment to illness, in two groups of hypertensive patients. Based on the clinical judgment of physicians, supported by a statistical analysis of blood pressure readings, 15 controlled and 15 uncontrolled hypertensives formed the sample. Compliance was evaluated with the Standardised Compliance Questionnaire, based on the Health Belief Model. There was no significant difference between the groups in health beliefs affecting compliance, calling into question the utility of measures based on the Health Belief Model to predict compliance potential of hypertensives (although this assumes that patients were 'uncontrolled' because they were non-compliant, in spite of no independent measure of compliance). However, significant differences were found in several aspects of psychosocial adjustment to illness, as assessed on the Psychosocial Adjustment to Illness Scale (Derogatis, 1977). Uncontrolled hypertensives showed less illness-related adjustment. They reported significantly greater difficulties in their domestic environment, more disturbances in extended family relationships and more psychological distress. For the uncontrolled group, less adjustment to illness was significantly correlated with less compliance with medication. The authors conclude that to enhance compliance in hypertensive patients an assessment needs to be made of illness-related adjustment problems.

Given et al (1984) studied the effects of patient characteristics and beliefs on the response to behavioural interventions aimed at improving compliance with a hypertensive regime. Two approaches to modifying beliefs were incorporated into a teaching programme provided by nurses. Patients in the control group (n = 24) were given information on their disease and therapy. For the experimental group (n = 62), a problem-solving strategy was employed to identify behavioural deficits and to set goals related to the desired psychosocial and clinical outcomes. Instruments were devised by the researchers to examine beliefs about the severity of disease, the efficacy of therapy, commitment to taking medication and commitment to following a diet. The intervention was successful in lowering diastolic blood pressure and altering beliefs about medication, but not about diet or exercise. In the experimental group selected pre-test variables derived from the Health Belief Model, such as knowledge, beliefs about susceptibility to disease and benefits to be derived from treatment, were not successful in explaining patients' responses to the intervention. The behavioural intervention extended over 6 months and involved about 6 hours of one-to-one interaction with each patient. Gains appear modest for this investment. Information provided about the control group intervention is scanty.

Harper (1984) applied Orem's theoretical constructs of self-care to self-medication behaviours in elderly, hypertensive, black women. An attempt was made to evaluate the effectiveness of a self-care medication programme on knowledge of medication, health locus of control and self-medication behaviour. The experimental group (n = 30) participated in a self-medication programme, and the matched control group (n = 30) participated in a programme providing only general information about hypertension. The experimental programme initially improved knowledge of medication, perceived control over health and self-care behaviours compared with the control group. However, follow-up analysis revealed a diminishing effect on these variables, underlining the need for nurses to conduct further research in the area of self-care, health behaviour and nursing interventions over time.

Pender conducted two studies (1984, 1985) involving patients with hypertension. In both studies, 22 patients with uncomplicated essential hypertension received relaxation training in a series of 3-weekly group sessions, followed by individual monitoring sessions over a 6-week period. In the first study, the control group of 22 patients did not receive relaxation training but instead received individual attention by a nurse: their blood pressure was measured, weight obtained, diet reviewed and medical compliance discussed. The group instructed in relaxation had a significantly lower mean systolic (but not diastolic) blood pressure than the control group at 4-month follow-up. Patients reported that they had continued to practise regularly the relaxation taught. Pender notes that an unusual feature of the study was group rather than individual relaxation instruction, and that interaction among group members seemed to stimulate learning and regular practice of relaxation routines. Unfortunately, as the control group patients were seen individually, it is not possible to assess to what extent results were due specifically to relaxation training rather than merely to group interaction.

In the second study, the control group received blood pressure monitoring, weight checks and health counselling but no relaxation training. Again, the experimental patients met as a group while the controls received individual attention. The group instructed in relaxation training exhibited significantly lower anxiety, as measured on the State – Trait Anxiety Inventory, at 4-month follow-up than did the control group. After training, the relaxation group also scored significantly higher than the control group on beliefs in personal control of health and lower in beliefs that chance or luck affected health outcomes, as measured on the Multidimensional Health Locus of Control Scales. The groups did not differ in the extent to which they believed that other individuals (e.g. health professionals, family members, etc.) influenced their health status.

Craig (1985) sought to identify the most accurate indirect

measure of medication compliance in primary hypertension. A review of the literature had indicated that patient interview was the most accurate of the indirect measures of hypertension, but this accuracy was determined by using pill count as a standard for reliability, which is a method of questionable reliability. Craig's study used for comparison a newly developed direct measure of compliance, high pressure liquid chromatography, to detect excretion of the anti-hypertensive diuretic hydrochlorothiazide. A convenience sample of 40 subjects was interviewed, and data were collected by an interview schedule, blood pressure measurement, pill counts, urine analysis and hospital record review. The structured, pre-coded interview schedule was developed by the investigator to elicit reports about the level of compliance with pill-taking and to gather information about the patients' perceptions of and compliance with other aspects of the medical regimen.

Results indicated that the most sensitive and accurate measure of compliance was patient interview. This measure correctly classified 85% of patients as compliant or non-compliant. Craig notes that from blood pressure alone, four subjects (10%) would be labelled unfairly as non-compliers. The most likely explanation of this is under-treatment. Sixty per cent of the subjects verified as non-compliant had acceptable diastolic blood pressures, suggesting that they did not need as much medication as prescribed. Craig concludes that if patients are asked directly and in a non-threatening manner about their medication consumption, this approach will correctly classify the largest number of individuals. Assessment of non-compliance should not be made on blood pressure alone, particularly since the label carries such a negative connotation. Involvement in the study may have enhanced patient compliance.

An article by Dawson (1985) commences:

'One way that patients participate in their own health care is by providing information about themselves to their health care providers.'

The purpose of Dawson's study was to compare groups of hypertensive and diabetic patients with a control group with no known chronic illness, in terms of their perceptions of clinician empathy and the importance and difficulty of disclosing personal information. Previous research had suggested that hypertensive patients tend to screen out noxious stimuli as a behavioural response to their hyperactive vasopressor system. It was hypothesised that hypertensives would differ from the two other groups in perceiving less clinician empathy and attributing less importance, but greater difficulty, to self-disclosure. The sample consisted of 54 hypertensives, 47 diabetics and 115 control patients. Perceived clinician empathy was measured with the empathy scale of the Barrett-Lennard Relationship Inventory (Gurman, 1977). A patient self-disclosure questionnaire, previously designed by the author, was used to obtain a measure of how important and difficult patients thought it was to discuss information. The instrument contains items in the content areas of personal problems and feelings, responses to health care and lifestyle. Data collection was by postal questionnaire from volunteer subjects.

The empathy hypothesis was supported but the self-disclosure hypotheses were not. Hypertensive patients differed from the diabetic and control groups in perceiving the least clinician empathy and attributing the greatest importance to discussing their responses to health care. Dawson suggests that the two most clinically significant findings in her study were that all patient groups rated 'responses to health care' as the most important category of self-disclosure topics to discuss with their doctor, and that reported difficulty in this area was influenced by perception of clinician empathy. She writes:

> 'Possibly, nurses and physicians strongly committed to educating patients about how to live in a health-promoting or an illness-controlling manner may, by their very zeal and apparent expertise, inadvertently also communicate a lack of openness to patient ideas and reactions. For those nurses and physicians concerned with adherence issues and truly believing the importance of patients' participating in their own health or medical care, these findings suggest the need for self-evaluation.'

Powers and Jalowiec (1987) attempted to identify predictive variables of blood pressure control (physiological outcome) and adjustment to chronic illness (psychosocial outcome) in 450 hypertensive patients. Hypertension control was determined by physician judgment, supported by blood pressure measurement, and adjustment was assessed by the Psychosocial Adjustment to Illness Scale. Potential predictors of the outcome variables were measured by structured interview, from medical records and with instruments such as the Jalowiec Coping Scale, the Hypertension

Knowledge Test, the Health History Questionnaire (all developed for the study) and the Multidimensional Health Locus of Control Scale. The findings were used to construct a profile of the well-controlled, well-adjusted hypertensive patient.

Well-controlled patients had better health adjustment scores, were more satisfied with health care, knew what to do about medication side-effects, had been on medication longer and had lower blood pressure readings. Well-adjusted patients had fewer hypertension-related problems, tended to be well-controlled, knew about medication side-effects, were less pessimistic and less likely to worry, and felt that their health was under their own control. The authors suggest that awareness of factors important in predicting control and adjustment outcomes in hypertension can be used to tailor interventions and facilitate patient teaching. Too often, professionals fail to take into account the diversity of factors that have an impact on the patient's response to illness in terms of physiological and psychosocial outcome.

Mann and Sullivan (1987) examined the effect of two systematically designed instructional programmes on the achievement and maintenance of a reduced dietary sodium intake in 66 adult hypertensives. Subjects were randomly assigned to one of three groups:

1. task-centred instruction;
2. task-centred instruction plus goal-setting and self-monitoring;
3. no structured teaching (control group).

All subjects were seen individually once a week for 6 weeks. Outcome variables, measured 6 weeks after pre-test and again 3 months later, were achievement test scores, 24-hour recall of dietary intake and 24-hour urinary sodium excretion. Multivariate analysis of covariance revealed significant effects for both instructional programmes ($p < 0.001$). However, the hypothesis that the addition of goal-setting and self-monitoring would result in significantly greater change than that achieved by the task-centred instructional programme alone was not supported. The authors note that reduction in dietary sodium is 'widely recommended' for hypertensive patients but provide no prior evidence for its efficacy in lowering blood pressure. This study showed a significant treatment effect on diastolic blood pressure ($p < 0.01$).

CHRONIC RESPIRATORY DISORDERS

Studies on respiratory disorders tended to concentrate on physiological, as opposed to psychosocial, adaptations to illness.

Sitzman et al (1983) studied four patients with chronic obstructive airways disease. A 4-week, thrice-weekly training programme was implemented in an attempt to promote a voluntary reduction in respiratory rate with a complementary increase of tidal volume. The main component of the programme was biofeedback, and improvement obtained was maintained over a 4-week period. This was a preliminary study only, which explains the small sample, and it is not known how long improvement was maintained.

Sexton and Munro (1986) studied the impact of a husband's chronic respiratory illness on the spouse's life, based on evidence from the literature that a supportive significant other person is probably the single most important factor in adjusting to a chronic illness. The sample consisted of 76 married women. The husbands of 46 had chronic obstructive airways disease (COAD), the remaining 30 husbands did not have a chronic illness. Data were collected by a postal questionnaire containing sections on biography, illness impact, subjective stress and life satisfaction.

Results indicated that wives whose husbands had COAD had high levels of subjective stress and low life satisfaction compared to wives in the other group. Wives of COAD patients rated their health as significantly poorer than did the other wives. The researchers note that current measures of life stress do not include chronic illness of the spouse as a stressor. Nurses need to focus attention on patients' spouses to help them to attain the best quality of life possible within the limits set by their spouse's illness and disability. Wives whose husbands were not chronically ill were selected on the basis of their membership in social and church groups, which may have biased results.

A series of studies by Janson-Bjerklie and colleagues (1986a, b, 1987; Carrieri and Janson-Bjerklie, 1986) looked at the sensations of pulmonary dyspnoea in patients with various respiratory chronic disorders. In one study (1986a) the researchers hypothesised that social support would have a buffering effect on dyspnoea. However, dyspnoea *increased* with increased social support.

A survey was conducted by Hautman (1987) into 'self-care

responses' to respiratory illness among Vietnamese people in the USA. The subjects were not all patients, and respiratory illness included acute conditions. This study is mentioned because of Hautman's interesting idea that culture-dependent 'folk practices' should be destigmatised by relabelling them 'self-care practices'.

OTHER AND MULTIPLE CHRONIC CONDITIONS

Craig and Edwards (1983) present a conceptual model of the process of adaptation in chronic illness. This is based on Lazarus' concept of appraisal (1966) and the idea that continuous appraisal and reappraisal of the individual's progress towards the goal of adaptation is required by the individual, his family and the nurse. The focus of this model is the chronically ill individual and his family; the goal is adaptation; the process is caring, which facilitates movement towards the goal. The paper concludes with a detailed list of goals and nursing strategies for:

- helping the individual and his family to achieve a realistic (re)appraisal of the situation;
- helping the individual and his family to identify appropriate and helpful adaptive tasks;
- facilitating the development and utilisation of beneficial coping behaviour.

Sexton (1983) looked at some methodological issues in chronic illness research, mostly dealing with the difficulty of obtaining access to representative samples and the danger of interviewers disrupting established coping patterns. She concludes:

> 'Designing the greatly needed studies of the chronically ill or aged will require considerable knowledge on the part of investigators as well as in sample acquisition and data collection. The study of chronic illness cannot be avoided simply because it is difficult, for the problems of the chronically ill and the aged will increasingly fall to nursing and nursing will need to develop theory to address them.'

Foxall et al (1985) examined the adjustment patterns of 30 chronically ill, middle-aged persons and their spouses, on the basis that learning to live with a chronically ill person is as important as learning to live with the illness. How the family responds will affect its capacity in health matters and its quality of life. The authors note that scientific evidence of the impact of chronic illness on family members is sparse. Most research on chronic illness has focused on the sick individual. Foxall et al's exploratory survey was designed to determine similarities and differences in the adjustment patterns of chronically ill patients in the community and their spouses, and to describe factors associated with such adjustment. Primary diagnosis of the ill subjects included arthritis (12), hypertension (7), cardiovascular accident (5), chronic obstructive lung disease (4) and cardiovascular disease (2). Couples from a convenience sample were interviewed in their homes using a Life Satisfaction Index, a Multidimensional Functional Assessment Questionnaire, and a Disability Classification Index.

No significant difference between chronically ill subjects and their spouses was found on overall adjustment scores. This finding was interpreted as a reflection of the impact of chronic illness on both partners. Specifically, the findings suggested that the ill subject was more concerned with self-esteem, social support, developmental tasks and the means of obtaining more money, whereas spouses were more concerned with the result of not having enough money. Major discriminating variables between low and high adjustment in the ill group were gender (female = lower), financial concerns, illness duration and level of disability, social isolation and loneliness. However, only desire for more social contact and disability level significantly correlated with adjustment. In the spouse group major discriminating variables between the low and high adjusters were loneliness, perception of illness duration and disability of the affected partner, financial concerns and age (older = lower). For this group all major discriminating variables except age correlated significantly with adjustment. Results are limited by the sample size, and the authors stress the exploratory nature of their study.

Foxall et al suggest that is is becoming increasingly important for nurses to have an understanding of how the chronically ill person and spouse adjust to daily living, and that this understanding would help in the planning of individualised family care and the promotion of positive adjustment patterns. Given that longer illness duration and level of disability were frequently associated with low adjustment in the ill subjects, nurses should carefully assess these variables. Assisting the person to maximise physical capabilities should lead to improved adjustment. Spouses may be helped through interventions to decrease their feelings of social isolation and loneliness. Improvements in the adjustment of the ill person may be reflected in improved adjustment of the partner. Attention also needs to be given to couples' financial concerns.

Lowery and Jacobson (1985) studied the causes that patients with diabetes, hypertension and arthritis give for their perceived success or failure in coping with the illness, and for the relationship of these causes to illness outcomes and expectations. This study built on the results of the exploratory study with arthritics reviewed above (Lowery et al, 1983) but this time had a much larger sample and a less complex design. All available arthritic, diabetic and hypertensive patients attending the clinics at a large teaching hospital over a 9-month period were asked to participate: 95% agreed to do so (n = 296). Patients were interviewed by trained nurses and asked to rate on a four-point scale how well they were doing with their illness. They were then asked an open-ended question on the causal attributions of their illness and rated 10 possible causative statements on a five-point scale. The causal replies were rated as in the previous study.

Results indicated that patients tended to attribute success internally and failure externally, and so provide partial support for attribution theory and its propositions. However, future expectations were not mediated by the stability of causes given for current success or failure: even those who were doing poorly and who gave a stable cause were optimistic about their future. Subjects who perceived themselves as failing to cope showed little conviction about causative factors for their illness. As length of time since diagnosis increased, subjects attributed less control over their health to their own actions. Overall, the results suggest that factors other than causal dimensions mediate patients' responses to their illness. These factors require investigation, prior to which caution should be exercised in proposing attribution-retraining programmes.

Observation of a population of patients with chronic heart failure suggested that some patients adapted to their disease more effectively than others. This difference in response did not appear to be related to the severity of the disease but, rather, to psychosocial variables, including a positive future orientation. Rideout and Montemuro (1986) investigated the relationship between the variables of hope and morale, the individual's level of function and the physiological status of that individual. Twenty-three out-patients were interviewed using the Beck Hopelessness Scale, the Philadelphia Geriatric Centre Morale Scale and an adapted version of the McMaster Health Status Index (to assess social function). Physiological status was determined by clinical signs and symptoms on a scale previously devised to measure severity of heart failure, although doubts about its sensitivity were expressed by the researchers.

The original hypothesis that patients with higher hope and morale scores would have higher physical function irrespective of severity of disease was not supported. There was a moderate-to-good correlation between hope, morale and social function. This raised the question of whether subjects who were more social remained more hopeful, or whether those who had more expectations for the future and a higher level of morale maintained or developed more social contacts. The authors suggest that nursing interventions contributing to the enhancement of hope for the future and active participation with others are indicated. Possible interventions include helping the patient to set realistic goals, encouraging the active involvment of the patient in decision-making related to his current health status, and directing the patient's thoughts beyond his present status to the future. Nurses need to trust the will to live of the patients with whom they work.

Pollock (1986) set out to investigate physiological and psychosocial adaptation of adults with chronic illness. She examined the 'hardiness characteristic': a specific set of attitudes towards challenge, commitment and control that is thought to mediate the stress response. She related these attitudes, measured by the Health-Related Hardiness Scale (Pollock, 1984), to physiological and psychosocial adaptation in 60 subjects with a chronic illness. There were three equally sized groups of patients, with either IDD, essential hypertension or rheumatoid arthritis. Hardiness was significantly correlated with physiological adaptation for the diabetic group, but not for the hypertensives or arthritics. There was no significant correlation between hardiness and psychosocial adaptation for any group. Physiological and psychosocial adaptation were found to be independent of each other in this study.

Cameron and Gregor (1987) reviewed the literature on treatment compliance in chronic illness, looked at from the health professional's and the patient's perspectives. In essence, a patient with chronic disease assesses recommended treatments according to how well they can be fitted into his everyday routine. Strategies for improving compliance are discussed, and the authors conclude that contingency contracting has great potential for development by nurses working with the chronically ill. Contracting encourages patient participation in care and provides the practitioner with an opportunity to understand the patient's motives, demands and priorities, so that an appropriate regime can be worked out. Specific, well-defined goals are established, and reinforcement for goal attainment is provided. They suggest that 'patient participation can include family participation because improved compliance is associated with a supportive family'. The mechanics of contingency contracting, and its potential disadvantages, are not discussed.

The remaining study in this group (Hoskins et al, 1986) looked at the concept of nursing diagnosis in the chronically ill and explored a methodology for clinical validation of such diagnoses.

4 | Discussion

COMMENT ON THE RESEARCH FINDINGS

The main impression gained from reviewing the active patient model is that supporting evidence for its claims is rather fragmentary (although perhaps not quite so fragmentary as my review would indicate). This, I suggest, is partly the result of a limited definition and conceptualisation of what being an active patient involves. Steele et al (1987), and many of the researchers they cite, view the active patient concept as relating primarily to doctor – patient interaction. Also, there appears to be an emphasis on behavioural interventions and tinkering with the mechanics of the patient – provider relationship. Participation is seen very much as a route to increased compliance and improved goal attainment. While such aims are laudable in themselves, one wonders if the ideal of patient autonomy has become submerged in the process.

Steele et al recommend that ideologically driven studies be replaced by research that is embedded in an articulated theory of patient behaviour per se. However, to construct a model of the active patient from the perspective of the doctor's surgery or out-patient clinic may be compared to describing a room on the basis of the view through a keyhole. The chances of gaining a non-fragmentary impression are rather low. As Conrad (1985) notes:

'Most people with illnesses, even chronic illnesses such as epilepsy, spend only a tiny fraction of their lives in the patient role.'

Surely, the experience of being a patient cannot be entirely separated from other, much more extensive, life experience, and the active patient must be described, initially at least, within this context.

On the other hand, to construct a complete and detailed picture of the active patient it is important to examine in detail individual aspects of health behaviour and interventions affecting this behaviour. So, the research described in chapter 2, in areas such as participation preferences and goal-setting, is very useful when correctly evaluated and applied, but it is probably wrong to expect a compilation of such studies to fit together into an overall model of the active patient.

By looking at a discrete body of nursing research, the importance attached to patient participation can be weighed relative to other concerns. Nursing research in chronic illness appears to demonstrate an interest in, and commitment to, the ideal of patient participation and a willingness to confront the problems of making it a reality.

Although many of the studies reviewed, in common with those in chapter 2, were conducted in out-patient settings, there was less emphasis on patient – provider – specifically patient – doctor – interaction and greater attention to the patient's experience of his illness and care. Physiological, psychological and socioeconomic variables were all considered in various studies, and sophisticated methodology, instruments and analysis were employed. Patients' families were often involved and their views, experience and quality of life regarded as important. Interventions to promote participation were not confined to issues of compliance. Studies that did look at patient compliance tended to stress the importance of the patient's perspective and the rationality of his or her decision-making. Some studies displayed methodological weaknesses of varying degrees of seriousness, partly due to the attempt to analyse the complexity of patient behaviour without reducing it to abstractions.

After an initial survey of research on the active patient model, the area of nursing research in chronic illness was selected as a second area to review because it seemed essential to choose the potentially most fruitful field if anything of value was to be located. It was, therefore, most encouraging to find that nurses appear to be meeting the challenge of participation in an holistic and family-centred way.

LIMITATIONS OF THE RESEARCH REVIEW

Only an overview of research in two areas is provided. Ganong (1987) discusses the criteria to be met by a good integrative review, and most of these standards are not met here. For instance, the articles discussed represent only a section of those available, and, particularly in the case of the active patient model, no objective basis for selection is given. Also, in most cases, insufficient information is provided to allow readers to examine the evidence and draw their own conclusions from studies. This account has not confined itself to experimental studies but has included qualitative, descriptive and theoretical material as well. Consequently, the review does not summarise the accumulated evidence of primary research adequately enough for truly valid conclusions to be drawn. However, this overview, attempting to trace the way in which the ideology of patient participation has been carried over into research, could be a useful starting point for a series of critical, integrative reviews, as discussed below.

The rationale of choosing two areas to review (the active patient and chronic conditions) may be questioned. Although such selection seemed justifiable on a theoretical basis, it may be that a different approach would have yielded more fruitful results. For instance, concentrating on the active patient model alone might have allowed more valid conclusions to be drawn about the extent of research in this field. An historical survey of research, paralleling that of Kaufmann (1983) on informed consent, might have provided useful information on the growing interest in various aspects of patient participation. Alternatively, looking at nursing research over a broader area of practice (e.g. psychiatry, paediatrics, district nursing, etc.) might have been valuable. Again, the present account could be used as a starting point for such a project.

The journals from which articles on chronic health problems were culled may not be the most appropriate ones if evidence of patient participation is sought. Specialised publications geared towards patient education, for example, *Diabetes Educator*, might be more useful.

Finally, the majority of the research discussed is American in origin, which may limit the generalisability of findings. Theory and research in chapter 2 relating to doctor – patient interactions may not be generalisable to nurse – patient interaction.

IMPLICATIONS FOR PRACTICE

It is not possible to draw detailed and specific implications for practice from such a limited review. Limitations are also imposed by the inconclusive or incomplete evidence provided by research in some areas. However, to a considerable extent, evidence from the nursing research tends to reinforce and extend the applicability of findings from the active patient model. Tentatively, the following general suggestions can be made:

- Patients have a preference for information and, slightly less markedly, for a role in decision-making. Nurses should assess and be guided by these preferences.
- Preference for active participation varies according to factors such as disease severity, available social support, age, etc. Nurses should assess preference for participation on an individual basis and reassess as circumstances change.
- The preference of patients' families for participation also needs to be elicited.
- Families may be under stress in their role as care-givers, and nurses can provide practical and emotional support to enhance further participation.
- It is probably valuable to discuss with patients their expectations and desired outcomes of care and to reach agreement on realistic objectives.
- Mutual goal-setting, and possibly contingency or self-contracting, may facilitate goal achievement and outcome of care.
- Measures such as Quality of Life may be more valuable than patient satisfaction for assessing the value of care.

More specific implications for practice were noted with the relevant studies. Perhaps the most important and prevalent theme is that patient participation can be facilitated through an accurate assessment of the preferences, expectations and perceived needs of the patient and his or her family.

SUGGESTIONS FOR FURTHER RESEARCH

Nurses can contribute to the development of knowledge in any area through theory development, primary research, secondary analysis of data and clinical investigation (Ganong, 1987).

Theory development

Steele et al (1987) write:

> 'The atheoretical nature of most of the research on patient autonomy has contributed to terminological confusion, non-comparable operational definitions, and at times to an inability to explain pertinent research findings.'

They urge investigators to substitute theory driven research programmes for those motivated by advocacy of a particular ideological stance. It may be erroneous to suppose that research can ever be divorced from its ideological framework (Rose and Rose, 1973), but at least this framework can be made explicit. Nurses seem to have gone some way towards incorporating ideals such as patient autonomy into their theory building but, as earlier sections have discussed, ambiguities remain to be addressed.

The concept of a continuum of participation might be developed to make it more comprehensively descriptive, and perhaps usefully predictive, of levels of patient and professional activity. From the research already undertaken, variables affecting level of participation appear to include type and severity of illness, age and socioeconomic status.

Primary research

Areas requiring attention include the following:

- Further development of reliable and valid measures of patient participation preferences.
- Investigation of information needs of different patient groups and sub-groups.
- Investigation of the active participation needs of different groups and sub-groups.
- Exploration of methods to tailor information and participation choices accordingly.
- Development of reliable, valid and appropriate outcome measures for various forms of participation.

Many areas would benefit from replication studies or adaptation of existing strategies to nurse – patient, rather than doctor – patient, situations.

Secondary analysis of data

Integrative reviews on individual aspects of patient participation could be undertaken. For instance, goal-setting would appear to lend itself to this treatment. To be worthwhile, such a review should meet the same standards of clarity, methodology and replication as good primary research. Ganong (1987) provides a useful discussion of criteria to be met by such reviews.

Clinical investigation

Brooking (1986) and Batehup (1987) suggest potentially fruitful lines of enquiry in the clinical situation. Steele et al call for research to be embedded in an articulated theory of patient behaviour per se. Nurses are well placed to study patient (and professional) behaviour and have made substantial contributions in this field. Such studies help to refine theory, get to grips with the difficulties in implementing strategies to improve participation, and keep nurses in touch with patient needs and preferences.

Research needs to be extended to all types of settings. Of particular interest recently have been descriptive accounts of units struggling to increase consumer input to care (e.g. Wilding et al, 1988). Situations such as these may lend themselves well to action research, providing support and guidance to nurses in implementing change.

Further research should build on work already undertaken. Researchers also need to re-appraise the fundamental tenets of patient participation in the light of critiques developed in recent years. The concluding chapter of this review raises some of the issues.

5 Patient participation re-examined

This concluding chapter concentrates on raising questions that require closer examination, rather than on attempting to offer solutions. Where possible, findings of the research review will be used to illustrate points arising from the theoretical literature.

THE USEFULNESS OF THE PATIENT PARTICIPATION CONCEPT

Patient participation is an inadequate concept in some respects. Most aspects of promoting participation seem to involve improving the social niceties of health-care transactions without altering the fundamental power structure. Brownlea (1987) suggests that although participation is seen as a way of broadening the range of inputs to a decision, in actual fact it may represent a kind of 'tokenism'. Rather than influencing the decision, it provides a platform for the acceptance of a decision made elsewhere in the system. As such, participation may validate or legitimate the status quo rather than promote change.

McEwen et al (1983), considering the allied concept of self-help, see it as addressing itself to the symptoms of the problem rather than to the causes. Instead of providing what is not provided by the state, perhaps groups should pressure the state into allotting them a fair share of resources. Of course, it could be said that self-help groups help to raise consciousness and that such campaigning may be part of their role. In some instances, this is made difficult by restrictions precluding organisations with charitable status from involvement in political activities.

Alternatively, the concept of patient participation may be

regarded as part of the process of medicalisation, whereby professionals are becoming involved in aspects of health for which self-care and treatment have always been the norm:

> '"Self-care" implies that it is care, in the medical sense, that one is giving to oneself which might otherwise, perhaps ideally, be given by a practitioner.' (Swenson, 1978)

LIMITATIONS OF THE CONSUMER APPROACH TO HEALTH

Kickbush (1981) writes:

> 'People are not just consumers of health care, they provide it themselves.'

Even in aspects of health care where professional services are involved, it is sometimes difficult for patients and clients to function as active consumers. Consumerism implies some degree of choice and equality in relationships, so that the consumer can withdraw his or her custom if the goods and services provided do not meet requirements. For patients who are seeking treatment for illness, there is often very little choice involved, even for those prepared to pay for the privilege. As Salvage (1985) notes, as well as implying choice and independence, health consumerism fits in with the private medical idea of customers and financial transactions. It fails to put across the model of partnership where patients and professionals work together for the patient's well-being. In addition, if we are already 'consumers', it may be easier to present the eventual privatisation of the health service as being in our own interests.

Patients are rarely equal partners in transactions and are often reluctant to press their case for information or alternative therapy. They may fear confrontation and being labelled as neurotic, a nuisance or unpopular. Doctors are regarded as powerful and prestigious, and the self-governing nature of the profession makes it difficult to gain a hearing for complaints or redress for damage (McEwen et al, 1983). In the case of nurses, patients are usually grateful for the care offered and tend to make allowances for shortcomings, which they attribute to the lack of physical amenities and to 'the system' in general (Altschul, 1983).

Consumers require information on which to base their

consumption decisions and to direct their lobbying activities. If real participation is extended to people outside the system, they should be treated, for the purposes of information-sharing, in the same way as those within the system. At present, there appears to be an inner system, which has enormous information resources, and an outer satellite system, which has only selective access to the information base (Brownlea, 1987). A distinct boundary does not necessarily exist at the patient – provider interface. For example, nurses may find themselves 'nursing in the dark' (Melia, 1982), with insufficient information to care for their patients or to keep them fully informed.

The consumerist movement has strengthened the resources that the general community can bring to bear in the processes of advocacy and participation (Kuhn, 1985). However, those with the time and money to devote to participation, and with organisational backing, are often the only ones actually doing so. This is also the case in the health-care arena. As noted in the case of patient participation groups and community health councils, the representativeness of participants is questionable (Levitt, 1980). The effect is compounded when participants are purposely selected, often on the basis of value-laden criteria. This selection can be seen at all levels, from political influence in the selection of members of health authorities and community health councils, to individual patients chosen for participation in their care on the basis of age, socioeconomic status or other, less tangible, criteria. This is a difficult problem to overcome. As observed, research seems to confirm the existing prejudices as to which patients wish to participate in health and are most likely to benefit from doing so.

THE EXTENT OF SELF-CARE

The idea of promoting patient participation leads to a tendency to neglect, or under-rate, the present extent of self-care in the community. Dunnell and Cartwright (1972) and Elliot-Binns (1973) estimated, on the basis of community surveys, that between 75 and 80% of all care is self-provided. Bradshaw (1977) estimated that, in Britain, 80-85% of all illnesses are managed without doctor consultation. Clymer et al (1984) reviewed several studies showing that the vast majority of symptom and illness episodes are self-managed. In a study by Banks et al (1975), only one symptom in 37 led to a professional consultation.

The literature also suggests that the practice of self-care is effective. Dunnell and Cartwright, and Elliot-Binns, found no difference in outcome between self-care and professional care. McEwen et al (1983) write:

> 'What is perhaps remarkable is not that most people treat themselves, but that this should be commented upon.'

The fact that such comment is necessary underlines the medicocentric view of patients as passive beings in need of professional 'activation' to participate in care. 'A view from the other side' (Stimson, 1974) regards patients as rational and capable individuals who have been incapacitated and deskilled by the system.

ECONOMY OR NEGLECT?

The emphasis on self-care, although it can be defended on ideological grounds, may result in a failure to provide sufficient statutory services. This is likely to be compounded by the move towards community care for the elderly, mentally ill and handicapped, and the practice of earlier discharge from general hospitals. Self-care may be a euphemism for cost-cutting and neglect, as Opit (1977) cogently suggests:

> 'domiciliary care for the elderly sick will be increasingly "economic" simply because the level of care provided becomes increasingly inadequate.'

The burden of care will fall on voluntary services, family carers and the patients themselves, leading to physical and financial hardship, loneliness and isolation. Self-care is often seen as a mutually exclusive alternative to professional care, which should not be the case (Muir Gray, 1985). Nor have professionals the right to promote a version of self-care leading to negative consequences for the sick and elderly (Ross, 1987).

To be effective, participation must be adequately and appropriately resourced, otherwise it will do nothing to alter the knowledge balance, skills balance and power balance of the community (Brownlea, 1987). Research of the type reviewed above is expensive to conduct and requires researchers with appropriate educational and professional preparation and expertise. There is no indication that interventions to promote effective and life-enhancing self-care will save money. In fact, rather the reverse is true. To improve patient well-being, in chronic illness for example, means moving from a situation of relative neglect to one where emotional, practical and financial support is offered to patients and their families.

Meyer (1985), a leading American consumer activist, notes that, in some senses, it is unfortunate that the move towards participation in health has occurred at a time of growing financial stringency. Being trapped into 'working together for cost-effective health care' can spell defeat at the outset. The central administration's definition of cost-effectiveness requires careful scrutiny because it often means an emphasis on eliminating or curtailing services that are vitally important to some sections of the population. Consumers should make their own decisions on what cost-effective health care involves and be prepared to defend their position vigorously.

Reviewing the report from Sir Roy Griffiths, *Care in the Community*, published on 15 March 1988, Stewart (1988) notes that the report's estimates for domiciliary care do not include the cost of GP visits, district nurse services or drugs on prescription. Yet these estimates are directly compared to estimates for other forms of care, which do include medical, nursing and drug costs.

EXTENDING THE SCOPE OF PARTICIPATION

High technology medicine may remain free of patient 'interference' because it is too difficult to understand. Doctors, and other professionals, will be able to retreat into their specialities to avoid the active patient. Only those at the primary care, patient – provider interface will be challenged to incorporate patient demands into their service.

Such a scenario would fit only too well into the continuum of participation based on Szasz and Hollender's models of the doctor – patient relationship (1956). Participation is seen as impossible or inappropriate for patients who are seriously ill. Yet it is the high technology hospital sector that is at the root of the escalation in costs, patient alienation and ineffectiveness (Brownlea, 1987).

Patients do require nurturing care when seriously ill, but in a strange environment where basic activities of living are no longer within their capability, participation in small ways may provide a valuable sense of personal control and achievement. Some level of participation should be possible for all but the unconscious patient. For instance, from personal experience, a patient in intensive care, ventilated via a tracheotomy, persistently refused mouth care by a nurse. However, given a little guidance, he was able and willing to perform this task himself, with very effective results. At the other end of the continuum, as the research review has indicated, patients with chronic health problems, and their carers, could benefit from increased professional support.

Recently, recognition has grown that patients may wish to participate in decision-making about their own resuscitation, and about treatment in the event of seriously incapacitating illness or accident. Anderson et al (1986) examined some of the recent literature on 'living wills' and surveyed 500 American nurses and 500 physicians to discover whether they had compiled their own living will. Twenty per cent of the respondents had a living will or something similar, and 48% were seriously interested in signing a living will, even if they had not already done so. However, such documents have dubious legal status, particularly in Britain. The subject is fraught with legal and ethical difficulties, but requires serious attention. Anderson writes:

> 'This declaration of personal wishes extends the right of informed consent to include the right of informed refusal. One might think of the living will as a method of self-care.'

A WHO document (World Health Organisation, 1987) examines the 'false antithesis' that seems to have arisen between hospitals and primary health care (PHC). In the hospital approach, improvement in health is often viewed as being beyond the power of the individual and in the realm of specialised providers of care; the service is thus professionally oriented and focuses on individual patients. The PHC approach, on the other hand, sees individuals and communities as being responsible for their own health; the service is community oriented. However, the need for community involvement applies to hospitals as much as to any other part of the health system.

Of course, the idea of 'self-care' is not entirely alien to the general hospital situation. Mullin (1980) describes how patients on medical and surgical wards are divided into three categories: total care, partial care and 'self-care'. 'Self-care' means that the ill adult only needs the bed made and perhaps a few medications administered. Focusing on tasks means that any needs that the 'self-caring' patient may have are obscured and he or she is deprived of nursing contact. If true participation is to be extended to all patients, this is the sort of problem that must be addressed. Fortunately, there is evidence of nurses beginning to confront and explore such issues (e.g. Brooking, 1986; Batehup, 1987).

THE PROFESSIONALISATION OF PARTICIPATION?

Concern has been expressed over the interest of health professionals in participation and self-care. Levin (1981) writes:

'Self-care is indigenous and ubiquitous and always has been. Its belated "discovery" by the health professions, some fear, may signify that the professions are responding to a threat by a social movement over which they have little or no control, a movement that could erode the present dominance of health by the medical profession in both the developing and the industrialised world. This may be a case of "If you can't beat them, join them".'

Or, as Geiger (1976) even more forcefully puts it, 'When the counter-culture develops something of value, the establishment rips it off and sells it back'.

There is a fine line between supporting an idea or strategy and controlling it. As Freire makes clear in *Pedagogy of the Oppressed* (1974), he who defines the problem controls the range of solutions. Swenson (1978) sees danger in the building of a professional self-care establishment, with its gurus, its 'scientific literature' and its apparatus of programmes to serve as handmaidens to medicine. Professionals have appropriated concerns, such as childbirth and death, that rightly belong to everyone. To reclaim these areas is the task of communities, whether the establishment concedes them or not. Because medicine has extended its domain in this way does not confer on it the right to supervise the 'transfer of skills' from practitioner to lay-person, as Levin et al (1977) suggest it should.

However, Levin and his associates consider that professional involvement in the development of participation need not inevitably lead to professional domination, if care is exercised. If professionals believe that patients should be encouraged and enabled to become as self-sufficient as possible in managing their health affairs, they must be prepared to allow, in day-to-day work, a true reduction in patient dependency, access to information, and the possibility of patients making their own decisions (and mistakes) about their care (Adcock, 1980).

Feuerstein (1980) defines participation as follows:

> 'a process in which a group or groups exercise initiative in taking action, stimulated by their own thinking and decision-making and over which they exercise specific controls.'

Here, the operative word is 'control' and in Feuerstein's context, it is seen to rest firmly with lay-people.

PROMOTING PARTICIPATION – THE BEST PLACE TO BEGIN

More involvement when individuals are well might be the best way to prepare for effective *patient* participation. Unfortunately, it has been found difficult to interest people in health matters before they recognise an actual, or potential, personal health problem (Richardson and Bray, 1987). This situation may be changing with the growing interest in fitness and well-being, and perhaps change can be facilitated by more imaginative forms of health education (Kickbush, 1981). Kickbush suggests three main lines of strategy:

1. Raising individual consciousness and knowledge about health and illness, about the body and its functions, and about prevention and coping.
2. Raising competence and knowledge in the use of the health-care system and providing an understanding of its functioning.
3. Raising awareness about social, political and environmental factors that influence health.

Also, specific preparation for participation might be less effective than a general improvement in educational levels and social equality. One of the most consistent research findings appears to be that preference for, and actual participation in, decision-making varies with social, educational and demographic factors. Whether this depends on the orientation of patient or provider, or both, the best way out may not be by tinkering with the mechanics of interaction but by stimulating broader social change.

At the level of promoting community involvement in health, many serious and sustained attempts have ended in disappointment (World Health Organisation, 1987). Among the reasons given for this are:

- People have not always been encouraged to think and choose for themselves and have, therefore, become used to 'solutions' being imposed on them by experts.
- Not enough effort and imagination have been devoted to structuring the health service so that people can participate in more than just token ways.

It would seem from this that people who have been consistently encouraged to 'think for themselves' will be the ones prepared to participate. Similarly, health-care providers require 'imagination' and the encouragement to apply it to their work. This all suggests inputs in terms of education and the provision of opportunities for development of a strong sense of personal worth and effectiveness, for both consumers and providers. To be effective, perhaps partnerships really do need to be between those with some fundamental basis of equality.

POLITICAL IMPLICATIONS

Kennedy (1981) writes:

> 'Medicine is, at bottom, a political enterprise. The choices we make as a society about how we govern ourselves, the values we espouse, dictate the kind of health we have, the kind of medical care we make available.'

The issues raised by aspects of patient participation can be regarded as intensely political (McEwen et al, 1983). At the two extremes, there is pressure for radical change, but arising from different motives. On the far left, people are seeking to institute their own medical services outside the establishment. On the right, there are demands for de-escalation of statutory services on the grounds that such provision encroaches on the freedom of the individual.

If participation at every level of health care is to be effective, the political will of society must be behind it so that appropriate structures and relationships can be set up to give people access to the key resources of power, knowledge and skill (Brownlea, 1987). However, there can be tension between national and local policies, as Klein (1978) points out. Implementation of national policies requires centralised control, whereas effective participation by workers and consumers necessitates flexibility, local democracy and diffusion of control.

Many feel that the structure of the NHS, from an administrative point of view, makes any real participation very limited. Draper et al (1976) comment thus on the 1974 reorganisation of the NHS:

> 'The primary obligation of both providers and recipients is to know their place, and to follow the orders of their betters, that is, the providers in the case of patients, and hierarchical superiors in the case of providers . . . In such systems, people cannot participate in making the decisions which affect them directly.'

There is little to suggest that the situation has radically altered since, in detail or in orientation.

CHANGING THE SYSTEM

Radcliffe-Brown (1959) differentiates two kinds of social change:

1. *Readjustment.* This occurs in the normal course of events, at a marriage, for instance. A re-grouping takes place and there is, in some sense, a change. On the other hand, the event has conserved and reinforced the traditional patterns of society.
2. *Change of type.* In this, the structural form of society alters.

Professionals within the existing structure are committed to change of some sort: for example, the introduction of new drugs, the move towards community care, etc. However, these changes can be seen as 'readjustments' without any alteration in the general roles, status and rules (McEwen, 1983). Freidson (1984), for instance, argues that the medical profession has retained essential political, institutional and decision-making control over the way the health-care system operates in most countries.

This is not to deny that readjustments are necessary and could prove extremely helpful in promoting patient participation. For instance, improvements in inter-professional relationships might produce an atmosphere in which professionals with differing skills and experience are accorded more respect and their potential contributions recognised. This would leave the way open for similar recognition to be extended to the contribution of patients and clients (Salvage, 1985).

If the structural form of the health service is to alter, a development that may be conducive to increased consumer participation is extension of the role of the nurse. There are signs that nurses are preparing themselves for new responsibilities and that partnership with consumers is very much a priority. To give only two examples:

The nurse practitioner

Barbara Stilwell's research into the acceptability of nurse practitioners to patients produced evidence that nurses can be effective resources for patients. Nurses can make it easier for patients to ask questions; they can answer patient questions and help them to cope with their disease, whether it is physical, social or emotional:

> 'The focus of my consultation is not the patient's illness, but her ability to cope with it − what does she need in the way of information or medication or further medical help for a good recovery from this illness, and what will help her to stay well in the future?'

Patients were found to be extremely competent in deciding which complaints to present to the nurse practitioner (Stilwell, 1986).

Health visiting and school nursing

A report from the Health Visitors' Association, *Bridging the Gap* (1988), discusses consumer participation in health visiting and the school nursing service. It concludes that there is major potential for expanding and changing ways of service delivery and that more research is needed in this area. Margaret Ayton, a health promotion facilitator in primary care, who worked on drawing up the report, states:

> 'Practitioners need to be supported in developing new initiatives. The goal is genuine handing over of power to the consumer.' (*Nursing Times*, **84**(9):8)

McEwen et al (1983) argue that, if nurses are to extend their traditional role and become involved in promoting patient participation, they will have to clarify their own position with regard to the various nursing duties and functions they are prepared to perform. However, while critical self-examination is often fruitful, it can sometimes impede progress. Clay (1987) suggests a way forward:

> 'Rather than look for a grand philosophy for the parameters of nursing, I believe it is important to look at the areas where nurses are playing an extended role, to develop that role and consolidate it.'

CONCLUDING REMARKS

Steele et al (1987) see the active patient concept as part of a dialectic that has waxed and waned for two centuries, in synchrony with societal interest in autonomy, self-direction and personal responsibility. Brownlea (1987) also regards participation as 'tidal' in its behaviour. Sometimes the pull is strongly ideological in nature, sometimes the direct result of structural breakdown and sometimes because certain groups in the population may be particularly hurt, either economically or in terms of the level of their health.

The one thing that seems fairly certain is that participation is a demand that will not go away. The challenge has been extended to nurses to play a leading role in meeting this demand. For instance, Meyer (1985) writes:

> 'As the members of the health care team who have probably been the most responsive to patients, nurses can take the lead in bridging the communication gap between consumers and providers.'

Kuhn (1985), founder of America's Gray Panthers, says 'Nurses and patients – together we can heal the sick health care system'. In her view, a coalition of nurses and patients would have enormous potential for bringing about the social and political change necessary for an improved system of care.

However, as discussed, it is all too easy for participation to become part of a social rhetoric, or even just a cliché. The evidence for improved health outcomes from patient participation is suggestive but incomplete and far from conclusive. Also, it may be dangerous to romanticise people – particularly the most needy –

and create unrealistic expectations of what they can do for and by themselves. This can contribute to the shaping of a cynical attitude towards the contribution of people to their own welfare (Madan, 1987). An alternative is to suggest that nothing can be done without radical change to the health-care system.

As in most situations, the middle position probably holds the most promise. Increasing patient participation may help to overcome a sense of dependency and powerlessness and to begin to foster new working relationships between providers and consumers, based on partnership. With further research and application to practice, this goal should be within reach. Then, Richardson and Bray suggest:

'The benefits from this participation are not solely in the changes introduced ... Its importance lies in a slowly changing climate of opinion about the appropriate roles of the providers and receivers of care.'

Given time, this changing climate of opinion may, in turn, generate the pre-conditions for structural change (Navarro, 1976). Or, as Stilwell (1986) writes:

'the most lasting and revolutionary changes paradoxically do not come from revolution at all, but through the gradual evolution of ideas and attitudes until a new level or awareness demands change.'

References

Adcock M U (1980) The rationale and application of a needs assessment in patient education. In: *Patient Education: An Enquiry into the State of the Art*, Squyres W (ed.). New York: Springer.

Alexy B (1985) Goal setting and health risk reduction. *Nursing Research*, **34**: 283–288.

Altschul A T (1983) The consumer's voice: nursing implications. *Journal of Advanced Nursing*, **8**: 175–183.

Anderson G C, Walker M A H, Pierce P M and Mills C M (1986) Living wills: do nurses and physicians have them? *American Journal of Nursing*, **86**(3): 271–275.

Auerbach S M, Martelli M F and Mercuri L G (1983) Anxiety, information, interpersonal impacts, and adjustment to a stressful health care situation. *Journal of Personality and Social Psychology*, **44**(6): 1284–1296.

Auerbach S M, Kendall P C, Cuttler H F and Levitt N R (1976) Anxiety, locus of control, type of preparatory information, and adjustment to dental surgery. *Journal of Consulting and Clinical Psychology*, **44**(5): 809–818.

Averill J R (1973) Personal control over aversive stimuli and its relationship to stress. *Psychological Bulletin*, **80**: 286–303.

Avery-Jones F (1978) Getting the National Health Service back on course. *British Medical Journal*, **2**: 5–9.

Bailey J T and Claus K E (1975) *Decision Making in Nursing*. St Louis: C V Mosby.

Baly M E, Robottom B and Clark J M (1987) *District Nursing*, 2nd edn. London: Heinemann Nursing.

Bandura A (1977) *Social Learning Theory*. Englewood Cliffs, New Jersey: Prentice-Hall.

Bandura A (1986) *Social Foundations of Thought and Action: A Social Cognitive Theory*. Englewood Cliffs, New Jersey: Prentice-Hall.

Banks M H, Beresford S A A, Morrell D C, Waller J J and Watkins C J (1975) Factors influencing demand for primary medical care in women aged 20–44 years: a preliminary report. *International Journal of Epidemiology*, **4**(3): 189–195.

Barsky A J (1976) Patient heal thyself: activating the ambulatory medical patient. *Journal of Chronic Disease*, **29**: 585–597.

Batehup L (1987) *Relative's Participation in the Care of the Stroke Patient in*

General Medical Wards. Submitted for MSc thesis, Department of Nursing Studies, University of London.

Beauchamp T and Childress J (1979) *Principles of Biomedical Ethics.* New York: Oxford University Press.

Beck A T (1967) *Depression: Clinical, Experimental and Theoretical Aspects.* New York: Hoeber.

Becker M H (ed.) (1974) *The Health Belief Model.* Thorofare, New Jersey: Charles B Slack.

Beech B L (1988) *Who's Having Your Baby? A Health Rights Handbook for Maternity Care.* London: Camden Press.

Benarde M A and Mayerson E W (1978) Patient – physician negotiation. *JAMA,* **239:** 1413–1415.

Berg A O and LoGerfo J P (1979) Potential effect of self-care algorithms on the number of physician visits. *New England Journal of Medicine,* **300:** 535–537.

Boston Women's Health Book Collective (1971) *Our Bodies, Ourselves: A Book By and For Women.* New York: Simon and Schuster.

Bowling A (1981) *Delegation in General Practice: A Study of Doctors and Nurses.* London: Tavistock.

Bradshaw J S (1977) British barefoot doctors? *Royal Society of Health Journal,* **97**(4): 159–164.

Brehm J W (1966) *A Theory of Psychological Reactance.* New York: Academic Press.

British Medical Journal (1986) For debate: patients' access to personal health information. *British Medical Journal,* **292**(6515): 254–256.

British United Provident Association (BUPA) (1984) *The BUPA Manual of Fitness and Well-Being.* London: MacDonald.

Brody D S (1980) The patient's role in clinical decision-making. *Annals of Internal Medicine,* **93:** 718–722.

Brooking J (1984) The art of applying the act. *Nursing Mirror,* **159**(10), supplement, pp.i–viii.

Brooking J I (1986) *Patient and Family Participation in Nursing Care: The Development of a Nursing Process Measuring Scale.* PhD thesis, Department of Nursing Studies, University of London.

Brown G W and Harris T (1978) *Social Origins of Depression: A Study of Psychiatric Disorder in Women.* London: Tavistock.

Brownlea A (1987) Participation: myths, realities and prognosis. *Social Science and Medicine,* **25**(6): 605–614.

Brownlea A, Taylor C, Landbeck M, Wisharat R, Nalder G and Behan S (1980) Participatory health care: an experimental self-helping project in a less advantaged community. *Social Science and Medicine,* **14D:** 139–146.

Burckhardt C S (1985) The impact of arthritis on quality of life. *Nursing Research,* **34**(1): 11–16.

Burnham P J (1966) Letter on medical experimentation on humans. *Science,* **152:** 448–450.

Burrows-Hudson S (1985) Assuring informed choice: a literature review. *ANNA Journal,* **12**(3): 177–180.

Byers P H (1985) Effect of exercise on morning stiffness and mobility in patients with rheumatoid arthritis. *Research in Nursing and Health,* **8**: 275–281.

Cameron R and Best J A (1987) Promoting adherence to health behaviour change interventions: recent findings from behavioral research. *Patient Education and Counseling,* **10**: 139–154.

Cameron K and Gregor F (1987) Chronic illness and compliance. *Journal of Advanced Nursing,* **12**: 671–676.

Carrieri V K and Janson-Bjerklie S (1986) Strategies patients use to manage the sensation of dyspnoea. *Western Journal of Nursing Research,* **8**(3): 284–305.

Cartwright A and O'Brien M (1976) Social class variations in health care and in the nature of general practitioner consultations. In: *The Sociology of the NHS,* Stacey M (ed.). Sociological Review Monograph,No. 22, pp.77–98.

Cassell E (1976) Disease as an 'it': concepts of disease revealed by patients' presentation of symptoms. *Social Science and Medicine,* **10**: 43–46.

Cassileth B R, Zupkis R V, Sutton-Smith K and March V (1980) Information and participation preferences among cancer patients. *Annals of Internal Medicine,* **92**: 832–836.

Castledine G (1981) The nurse as the patient's advocate: pros and cons. *Nursing Mirror,* **153**(20): 38–40.

Childress J F (1979) Paternalism and health care. In: *Medical Responsibility,* Robison W L and Pritchard M S (eds.) Clifton, New Jersey: Humana Press.

Clay T (1987) *Nurses: Power and Politics.* London: Heinemann Nursing.

Clement-Jones V (1985) Cancer and beyond: the formation of BACUP. *British Medical Journal,* **291**(6501): 1021–1023.

Clymer R, Baum A and Krantz D S (1984) Preferences for self-care and involvement in health care. In *Handbook of Psychology and Health, Vol. iv: Social Psychological Aspects of Health,* Baum A, Taylor S E and Singer J E (eds.). Hillsdale, New Jersey: Lawrence Earlbaum Associates.

Coleman V (1986) *The Patient's Companion: How to Get Good Health Care,* 2nd edn. London: Corgi Books.

Community Health Initiatives Resource Unit and London Community Health Resource (1987) *Guide to Community Health Projects.* London: CHIRU/LCHR.

Conduct and Utilization of Research in Nursing (CURN) Project, Michigan Nurses Association (1982) *Mutual Goal Setting in Patient Care.* New York: Grune and Stratton.

Connelly C E (1987) Self-care and the chronically ill patient. *Nursing Clinics of North America,* **22**(3): 621–629.

Conrad P (1985) The meaning of medications: another look at compliance. *Social Science and Medicine,* **20**(1): 29–37.

Conway-Rutkowski B (1982) The nurse: also an educator, patient advocate and counselor. *Nursing Clinics of North America,* **17**: 455–466.

Copp L A (1986) The nurse as advocate for vulnerable persons. *Journal of*

Advanced Nursing, **11**: 255–263.

Craig H M (1985) Accuracy of indirect measures of medication compliance in hypertension. *Research in Nursing and Health*, **8**:61–66.

Craig H M and Edwards J E (1983) Adaptation in chronic illness: an eclectic model for nurses. *Journal of Advanced Nursing*, **8**(5): 397–404.

D'Onofrio C (1980) Patient compliance and patient education. In: *Patient Education: An Enquiry into the State of the Art*, Squyres W (ed.) New York: Springer.

Davies C (1976) Experience of dependency and control in work: the case of nurses. *Journal of Advanced Nursing*, **1**: 273–282.

Dawson C (1985) Hypertension, perceived clinician empathy, and patient self-disclosure. *Research in Nursing and Health*, **8**: 191–198.

Dawson G (1983) Doctoring. *New Internationalist*, **127**: 18–19.

Demy N J (1971) Informed opinion on informed consent. *JAMA*, **217**: 696–697.

Department of Health and Social Security (1986a) *Neighbourhood Nursing – A Focus for Care: Report of the Community Nursing Review* (Chairman: Julia Cumberlege). London: HMSO.

Department of Health and Social Security (1986b) *Primary Health Care: An Agenda for Discussion*, Cmnd 9771. London: HMSO.

Derogatis L R (1977) *Psychosocial Adjustment to Illness Scale: Self-Report Version*. Baltimore: Clinical Psychometric Research.

DeVon H A and Powers M J (1984) Health beliefs, adjustment to illness, and control of hypertension. *Research in Nursing and Health*, **7**: 10–16.

Donaldson L J, Clarke M and Palmer R L (1983) Institutional care for the elderly: the impact and implications of the ageing population. *Health Trends*, **15**: 58–61.

Dracup K A and Meleis A I (1982) Compliance: an interactionist approach. *Nursing Research*, **31**(1):31–36.

Draper P, Grenholm G and Best G (1976) The organisation of health care: a critical view of the 1974 reorganisation of the National Health Service. In: *An Introduction to Medical Sociology*, Tuckett D (ed.) London: Tavistock.

Duin N and Jacka F (1987) *Health Help 1987/88*, 4th edn. London: Bedford Square Press/NCVO, for Thames Television.

Dunnell K and Cartwright A (1972) *Medicine Takers, Prescribers and Hoarders*. London: Routledge and Kegan Paul.

Dyer A R and Bloch S (1987) Informed consent and the psychiatric patient. *Journal of Medical Ethics*, **13**(1): 12–16.

Ehrenreich B and English D (1979) *For Her Own Good: 150 Years of the Experts' Advice to Women*. London: Pluto Press.

Eisenthal S and Lazare A (1976) Evaluation of the initial interview in a walk-in clinic. The patient's perspective on a 'customer approach'. *Journal of Nervous and Mental Disease*, **162**: 169–176.

Eisenthal S, Koopman C and Lazare A (1983) Process analysis of two dimensions of the negotiated approach in relation to satisfaction in the initial interview. *Journal of Nervous and Mental Disease*, **171**(1): 49–54.

Eisenthal S, Emery R, Lazare A and Udin H (1979) 'Adherence' and the negotiated approach to patienthood. *Archives of General Psychiatry*, **36**: 393–398.

Elliott-Binns C P (1973) An analysis of lay medicine. *Journal of Royal College of General Practitioners*, **23**: 255–264.

Faden R R, Becker C, Lewis C, Freeman J and Faden A I (1981). Disclosure of information to patients in medical care. *Medical Care*, **xix**(7): 718–733.

Fahrenfort M (1987) Patient emancipation by health education: an impossible goal? *Patient Education and Counseling*, **10**: 25–37.

Feuerstein M T (1980) Participatory evaluation: an appropriate technology for community health problems. *Contact*, **55**: 1–8.

Finesilver C (1978) Preparation of adult patients for cardiac catheterisation and coronary cineangiography. *International Journal of Nursing Studies*, **15**: 211–221.

Flinn M W (ed.) (1965) *Report on the Sanitary Conditions of the Labouring Population of Great Britain*, by Sir Edwin Chadwick, 1842. Edinburgh: Edinburgh University Press.

Foxall M J, Ekbert J Y and Griffith N (1985) Adjustment patterns of chronically ill middle-aged persons and spouses. *Western Journal of Nursing Research*, **7**(4): 425–444.

Freidson E (1961) *Patients' Views of Medical Practice*. New York: Russell Sage Foundation.

Freidson E (1970a) *Profession of Medicine: A Study of the Sociology of Applied Knowledge*. New York: Dodd, Mead and Co.

Freidson E (1970b) *Professional Dominance*. Chicago: Aldine.

Friedson E (1984) The changing nature of professional control. *American Review of Sociology*, **10**: 1–20.

Freire P (1974) *Pedagogy of the Oppressed*. New York: Herder and Herder.

Fry J (1966) *Profiles of Disease*. London: E and S Livingstone.

Fry J (1979) *Common Diseases: Their Nature, Incidence and Care*. Lancaster: MTP Press.

Fry J (ed.) (1983) *Common Dilemmas in Family Medicine*. Lancaster: MTP Press.

Fry J and Fryers G (1983) *The Health Care Manual: A Family Guide to Self-Care and Home Medicines*. Lancaster: MTP Press.

Ganong L H (1987) Integrative reviews of nursing research. *Research in Nursing and Health*, **10**: 1–11.

Gartner A and Reissman F (1976) Self help models and consumer-intensive health practice. *American Journal of Public Health*, **66**: 783–786.

Geiger J (1976) Quoted by Jencks S F, 'Problems in participatory health care', in *Self Help and Health: A Report*. New Human Services Institute, City University of New York, and *Social Policy*.

Gillie O and Mercer D (1982) *The Sunday Times Book of Body Maintenance*, 2nd edn. London: Mermaid Books.

Given C W, Given B A and Coyle B W (1984) The effects of patient characteristics and beliefs on responses to behavioral interventions for control of chronic diseases. *Patient Education and Counseling*, **6**(3): 131–140.

Given C W, Given B A, Gallin R S and Condon J W (1983) Development of scales to measure beliefs of diabetic patients. *Research in Nursing and Health*, **6**(3): 127–141.

Gostin L O (1983) *A Practical Guide to Mental Health Law*. London: National Association for Mental Health (MIND).

Graham O and Schubert W (1985) A model for developing and pretesting a multi-media teaching program to enhance the self-care behaviour of diabetes insipidus patients. *Patient Education and Counseling*, **7**(1): 53–64.

Green K E and Moore S H (1980) Attitudes toward self-care: a consumer study. *Medical Care*, **xviii**(8): 872–877.

Greenfield S, Kaplan S and Ware J E (1985) Expanding patient involvement in care. *Annals of Internal Medicine*, **102**: 520–528.

Griffiths R (1988) *Community Care: Agenda for Action*, A report to the Secretary of State for Social Services. London: HMSO.

Guglielmino L (1978) Development of the self-directed learning readiness scale, Doctoral dissertation, University of Georgia, 1977. *Dissertation Abstracts*, **38**: 6467A.

Gurman A S (1977) The patient's perception of the therapeutic relationship. In: *Effective Psychotherapy: A Handbook of Research*, Gurman A S and Razin A M (eds.). New York: Pergamon.

Hames A and Stirling E (1987) Choice aids recovery. *Nursing Times*, **83**(8): 49–51.

Harper D C (1984) Application of Orem's theoretical constructs to self-care medication behaviors in the elderly. *Advances in Nursing Science*, **6**(3): 29–46.

Haug M R (1980) The sociological approach to professional self regulation. In: *Regulating the Professions: A Public Policy Symposium*, Blair R and Rubin S (eds.). Lexington, Mass: Lexington Books.

Haug M R and Lavin B (1979) Public challenge of physician authority. *Medical Care*, **17**: 844–858.

Haug M R and Lavin B (1981) Practitioner or patient – who's in charge? *Journal of Health and Social Behavior*, **22**: 212–29.

Hautman M J (1987) Self-care responses to respiratory illnesses among Vietnamese. *Western Journal of Nursing Research*, **9**(2): 223–243.

Health Visitors' Association (1988) *Bridging the Gap*. London: HVA.

Hefferin E A (1979) Health goal setting: patient – nurse collaboration at VA facilities. *Military Medicine*, December; pp.814–822, quoted in Conduct and Utilization of Research in Nursing (CURN) Report, 1982.

Henderson V (1969) *Basic Principles of Nursing Care*, revised edition. Geneva: International Council of Nurses.

Hickey T (1986) Health behaviour and self care in later life. In: *Self Care and Health in Old Age*, Dean K, Hickey T and Holstein B (eds.). London: Croom Helm.

Hill L and Smith N (1985) *Self-Care Nursing: Promotion of Health*. Englewood Cliff, New Jersey: Prentice Hall.

Hoggett B (1984) *Mental Health Law*, 2nd edn. London: Sweet and Maxwell.

Hoskins L M, McFarland E A, Rudenfeld M G, Walsh M B and Schreier A M (1986) Nursing diagnosis in the chronically ill: methodology for clinical validation. *Advances in Nursing Science,* 8(3): 80–89.

Illich I (1973) The professions as a form of imperialism. *New Society,* 25(571): 633–635.

Illich I (1974) *Medical Nemesis: The Expropriation of Health.* London: Calder and Boyars.

Ingelfinger F J (1980) Arrogance. *New England Journal of Medicine,* 303: 1507–1511.

Janis I L and Rodin J (1979) Attribution, control, and decision-making: social psychology and health care. In: *Health Psychology.* Stone G D, Cohen F and Adler N E (eds.). San Francisco: Jossey-Bass.

Janson-Bjerklie S, Boushey H A, Carrieri V K and Lindsey A M (1986b) Emotionally triggered asthma as a predictor of airway response to suggestion. *Research in Nursing and Health,* 9: 163–170.

Janson-Bjerklie S, Carrieri VK and Hudes M (1986a) The sensations of pulmonary dyspnoea. *Nursing Research,* 35: 154–159.

Janson-Bjerklie S, Ruma S S, Stulbarg, M and Carrieri V K (1987) Predictions of dyspnoea intensity in asthma. *Nursing Research,* 36(3): 179–183.

X Janz N K, Becker M H and Hartmann P E (1984) Contingency contracting to enhance patient compliance: A review. *Patient Education and Counseling,* 5(4): 165 –178.

Jenny J (1986) Differences in adaptation to diabetes between insulin-dependent and non-insulin-dependent patients: implications for patient education. *Patient Education and Counseling,* 8(1): 39–50.

Jones A (1988) A level of independence. *Nursing Times,* 84(15): 55–57.

Katz A H and Bender E I (1976) *The Strength in Us: Self-Help Groups in the Modern World.* New York: New Viewpoints.

Katz J (1976) News from psychological centers. *Journal of Psychiatric Law,* 4: 315–325.

Kaufmann C L (1983) Informed consent and patient decision making: two decades of research. *Social Science and Medicine,* 17: 1657–1664.

Kearney B and Fleischer B (1979) Development of an instrument to measure exercise of self-care agency. *Research in Nursing and Health,* 2: 25–34.

Kennedy I (1978) The Mental Health act: a model response that failed. *World Medicine,* 13(12): 37, 38, 75, 76, 81, 82.

Kennedy, I (1981) *The Unmasking of Medicine.* London: George Allen and Unwin.

Kerrigan P (1983) The case for less patient participation (2). In *Common Dilemmas in Family Medicine,* Fry J (ed.). Lancaster: MTP Press.

Kickbush I (1981) Involvement in health: a social concept of health education. *International Journal of Health Education,* 24: 3–15.

Kingman S (1986) Medical research on trial. *New Scientist,* 111(1526): 48–52.

King's Fund (1986) Treatment of primary breast cancer: the second King's Fund Forum Consensus Statement. *British Medical Journal,* 293: 946–947.

Klein R (1978) Who decides? Pattern of authority. *British Medical Journal,* 2: 73–74.

Krantz D S, Baum A and Wideman M V (1980) Assessment of preferences for self-treatment and information in health care. *Journal of Personality and Social Psychology,* **39**(5): 977–990.

Kuhn M E (1985) Nurses and patients – together we can heal the sick health care system. *Nursing and Health Care,* **6**(7): 363–364.

Laborde J M and Powers M J (1985) Life satisfaction, health control orientation and illness-related factors in persons with osteoarthritis. *Research in Nursing and Health,* **8**: 183–190.

Lambertson E (1958) *Education for Nursing Leadership.* Philadelphia: J B Lippincott.

Lazare A, Eisenthal S and Wasserman L (1975) The customer approach to patienthood. *Archives of General Psychiatry,* **32**: 553–558.

Lazarus R S (1966) *Psychological Stress and the Coping Process.* Toronto: McGraw Hill.

Lazarus R S and Launier R (1978) Stress-related transactions between person and environment. In: *Perspectives in International Psychology,* Pervin L and Lewis M (eds.). New York: Plenum Press.

Levin L S (1981) Self-care in health: potentials and pitfalls. *World Health Forum,* **2**(2): 177–184.

Levin L S, Katz A H and Holst E (1977) *Self-Care: Lay Initiatives in Health.* London: Croom Helm.

Levitt R (1980) *The People's Voice in the NHS.* London: King Edward's Hospital Fund for London.

Lewis C E and Michnich M (1977) Contracts as a means of improving patient compliance. In: *Medication Compliance: A Behavioral Management Approach,* Barofsky I (ed.). Thorofare, New Jersey: Charles B Slack.

Like R and Zyzanski S J (1987) Patient satisfaction with the clinical encounter: social psychological determinants. *Social Science and Medicine,* **24**(4): 351–357.

Locke E A, Shaw K N, Saari L M and Latham G P (1981) Goal setting and task performance: 1969–1980. *Psychological Bulletin,* **90**: 125–152.

Locker D and Dunt D (1978) Theoretical and methodological issues in sociological studies of consumer satisfaction with medical care. *Social Science and Medicine,* **12**: 283–292.

Lomas H D (1981) Paternalism: medical or otherwise. *Social Science and Medicine,* **15F**: 103–106.

Lowery B J and Jacobsen B S (1985) Attributional analysis of chronic illness outcomes. *Nursing Research,* **34**(2): 82–88.

Lowery B J, Jacobsen B S and Murphy B B (1983) An exploratory investigation of causal thinking of arthritics. *Nursing Research,* **32**(3): 157–162.

McBride S (1987) Validation of an instrument to measure exercise of self-care agency. *Research in Nursing and Health,* **10**: 311–316.

McCall Smith A (1977) Comment on the RCN Code of Conduct. *Journal of Medical Ethics,* **3**: 122.

McCarthy M (1985) Taking control. *Nursing Times,* **81**(15): 52.

MacDonald J J (1983) Primary health care – health as a wedge. *Community Development Journal*, **18**(2): 164–166.

McEwen J (1985) Primary health care: the challenge of participation. In *Primary Health Care in the Making*, Laaser U, Senault R and Viefhues H (eds.). Heidelberg: Springer-Verlag.

McEwen J, Martini C J M and Wilkins N (1983) *Participation in Health*. London: Croom Helm.

McIntosh J (1974) Processes of communication, information seeking and control associated with cancer: a selective review of the literature. *Social Science and Medicine*, **8**: 167–187.

McIntyre K (1980) The Perry model as a framework for self care. *Nurse Practitioner*, **5**(6): 34, 35, 38.

McKeown T (1965) *Medicine in Modern Society*. London: George Allen and Unwin.

McKnight J (1977) Professionalised service and disabling health. In: *Disabling Professions*, Illich I, Zola I, McKnight J, Caplan J and Shaiken H (eds.). London: Marion Boyars.

McNeil B J, Pauker S G, Sox H C and Iversky A (1982) On the elicitation of preferences for alternative therapies. *New England Journal of Medicine*, **306**(21): 1259–1262.

Madan T N (1987) Community involvement in health policy: socio-structural and dynamic aspects of health beliefs. *Social Science and Medicine*, **25**(6): 615–620.

Mahler H (1982) The new look in health education. *Journal of the Institute of Health Education*, **20**(3): 5–12.

Mahler H (1983) Hospitals without walls. *Malawi Times*, 31 October.

Mann K V and Sullivan P L (1987) Effect of task-centered instructional programs on hypertensives' ability to achieve and maintain reduced dietary sodium intake. *Patient Education and Counseling*, **10**: 53–72.

Marsh G and Kaim-Caudle P (1976) *Team Care in General Practice*. London: Croom Helm.

Marston M V (1976) Nursing management of compliance with medication regimes. In *Medication Compliance: A Behavioural Management Approach*, Barofsky I (ed.). Thorofare, New Jersey: Charles B Slack.

Martin J F (1978) The active patient: a necessary development. *WHO Chronicle*, **32**: 51–57.

Martini C (1981) Discussion. *World Health Forum*, **2**: 197–198.

Mauksch I G and Miller M H (1981) *Implementing Change in Nursing*. St Louis: C V Mosby.

Melia K M (1982) 'Tell it as it is' – qualitative methodology and nursing research: understanding the student nurse's world. *Journal of Advanced Nursing*, **7**: 327–335.

Melnyk K A M (1983) The process of theory analysis: an examination of the nursing theory of Dorothea E Orem. *Nursing Research*, **32**(3):170–174.

Meyer L S (1985) Untangling communication lines to connect consumers and providers. *Nursing and Health Care*, **6**(7): 367–368.

Miller A (1985) Nurse/patient dependency – is it iatrogenic? *Journal of Advanced Nursing,* **10**: 63–69.

Miller T R (1974) One hundred cases of hemipelvectomy: a personal experience. *Surgical Clinics of North America,* **54**(4): 905–913.

Moughton M (1982) The patient: a partner in the health care process. *Nursing Clinics of North America,* **17**(3): 467–479.

Muir Gray J (1985) In: *New Initiatives in Self Health Care for Older People,* Glendinning F (ed.). Beth Johnson Foundation in association with Keele University and the Health Education Council.

Mullan F (1985) Seasons of survival: reflections of a physician with cancer. *New England Journal of Medicine,* **313**: 270–273.

Mullin V I (1980) Implementing the self-care concept in the acute care setting. *Nursing Clinics of North America,* **15**(1): 177–190.

Navarr O V (1976) *Medicine Under Capitalism.* New York: Prodist.

Nelson R O (1977) Assessment and therapeutic functions of self-monitoring. In *Progress in Behavior Modification, Vol. 5,* Hersen M, Eisler R M and Miller P M (eds.). New York: Academic Press.

Novack D H, Plumer R, Smith R L, Ochitill H, Morrow G R and Bennett J M (1979) Changes in physicians' attitudes toward telling the cancer patient. *JAMA,* **241**: 897–900.

O'Connel K A, Hamera E K, Knapp T M, Cassmeyer V L, Eaks G A and Fox M A (1984) Symptom use and self-regulation in type II diabetes. *Advances in Nursing Science,* **6**(3): 19–28.

O'Leary A (1985) Self-efficacy and health. *Behaviour Reseach and Therapy,* **23**(4): 437–451.

Oakley A (1984) What price professionalism? The importance of being a nurse. *Nursing Times,* **80**(50): 24–27.

Oermann M H, Doyle T H, Clark L R, Rivers C L and Rose V Y (1986) Effectiveness of self-instruction for arthritis patient education. *Patient Education and Counseling,* **8**: 245–254.

Office of Health Economics (1984) *Understanding the NHS in the 1980s.* London: OHE.

Oken D (1961) What to tell cancer patients: a study of medical attitudes. *JAMA,* **175**: 1120–1128.

Opit L J (1977) Domiciliary care for the elderly sick – economy or neglect? *British Medical Journal,* **1**: 30–33.

Orem D E (1985) *Nursing: Concepts of Practice,* 3rd edn. London: Collier Macmillan.

Parsons T (1951) *The Social System.* New York: The Free Press.

Pender N J (1984) Physiologic responses of clients with essential hypertension to progressive muscle relaxation training. *Research in Nursing and Health,* **7**: 197–203.

Pender N S (1985) Effects of progressive muscle relaxation training on anxiety and health locus of control among hypertensive adults. *Research in Nursing and Health,* **8**: 67–72.

Pendleton L and House W C (1984) Preferences for treatment approaches in medical care: college students versus diabetic outpatients. *Medical Care,* **22**(7): 644–646.

Pistorius G J (1983) The case for more patient participation (2). In: *Common Dilemmas in Family Medicine,* Fry J (ed.). Lancaster: MTP Press.

Player D (1983) Foreword to *The Health Care Manual: A Family Guide to Self-Care and Home Medicines,* Fry J and Fryers G (eds.). Lancaster: MTP Press.

Pollock S E (1984) Adaption to stress. *Texas Nursing,* **58**(10): 12–13, quoted in Pollock, 1986.

Pollock S E (1986) Human responses to chronic illness: physiologic and psychosocial adaption. *Nursing Research,* **35**: 90–95.

Pollock S E (1987) Adaption to chronic illness. *Nursing Clinics of North America,* **22**(3): 631–644.

Poteet G W, Reinert B and Ptak H E (1987) Outcome of multiple usage of disposable syringes in the insulin requiring diabetic. *Nursing Research,* **36**(6): 350–352.

Potter M (1981) Medication compliance – a factor in the drug wastage problem. *Nursing Times* Occasional Paper, **77**(5): 17–20.

Powers M J and Jalowiec A (1987) Profile of the well-controlled, well-adjusted hypertensive patient. *Nursing Research,* **36**(2): 106–110.

Powles J (1973) On the limitations of modern medicine. *Science Medicine and Man,* **1**: 1–34.

Pratt L (1971) *Family Structure and Effective Health Behavior: The Energised Family.* Boston: Houghton-Mifflin.

Pritchard P (1983) The case for more patient participation (1). In: *Common Dilemmas in Family Medicine* Fry J (ed.). Lancaster: MTP Press.

Pritchard P (1986) Why participate at all? In *Primary Health Care 2000,* Fry J and Hasler J (eds.). London; Churchill Livingstone.

Pritchard P (1986) *Patient Participation in General Practice: A Practical Guide to Starting a Group,* revised edition. Surbiton. National Association for Patient Participation.

Putnam S M, Stiles W B, Jacob M C and James S A (1985) Patient exposition and physician explanation in initial medical interviews and outcomes of clinic visits. *Medical Care,* **23**(1): 74–83.

Quill T E (1983) Partnerships in patient care: a contractual approach. *Annals of Internal Medicine,* **98**: 228–234.

Radcliffe-Brown A R (1959) *Method in Social Anthropology.* Chicago: University of Chicago Press.

Rakusen J and Phillips A (1978) *Our Bodies, Ourselves.* London: Allen and Lane.

Reiser S J (1978) *Medicine and the Reign of Technology.* Cambridge: Cambridge University Press.

Richardson A (1983) *Participation.* London: Routledge and Kegan Paul.

Richardson A (1984) *Working with Self-Help Groups: A Guide for Local Professionals.* London: Bedford Square Press.

Richardson A and Bray C (1987) *Promoting Health Through Participation.* London: Policy Studies Institute.

Rideout E and Montemuro M (1986) Hope, morale and adaption in patients with chronic heart failure. *Journal of Advanced Nursing*, **11**: 429–438.

Robb S S (1983) Beware the 'informed' consent. *Nursing Research*, **32**(3): 132.

Roper N, Logan W W and Tierney A J (1980) *The Elements of Nursing*. Edinburgh: Churchill Livingstone.

Rose S P R and Rose H (1973) Do not adjust your mind, there is a fault in reality – ideology in neurobiology. *Cognition*, **2**(4): 479–502.

Ross F M (1987) *Evaluation of a Drug Guide in Primary Care*. PhD thesis, Department of Nursing Studies, University of London.

Roter D L (1977) Patient participation in the patient – provider interaction, satisfaction and compliance. *Health Education Monographs*, **5**: 281–315.

Roth H P (1987) Measurement of compliance. *Patient Education and Counseling*, **10**: 107–116.

Rotter J B (1975) Some problems and misconceptions related to the construct of internal versus external control of reinforcement. *Journal of Consulting and Clinical Psychology*, **43**: 56–67.

Rovers R (1986) The merging of participatory and analytical approaches to evaluation: implications for nurses in primary health care programs. *International Journal of Nursing Studies*, **23**(3): 211–219.

Salvage J (1985) *The Politics of Nursing*. London: Heinemann Nursing.

Schroeder-Zwelling E and Hock E (1986) Maternal anxiety and sensitive mothering behavior in diabetic and non-diabetic women. *Research in Nursing and Health*, **9**: 249–255.

Schulman B A (1977) *Patient Participation in Treatment for Hypertension*. Unpublished doctoral dissertation, University of Michigan, quoted by Schulman, 1979.

Schulman B A (1979) Active patient orientation and outcomes in hypertensive treatment: application of a socio-organizational perspective. *Medical Care*, **17**(3): 267–280.

Schulz R (1976) The effects of control and predictability on the physical and psychological well-being of the institutionalized aged. *Journal of Personality and Social Pschology*, **33**: 563–573.

Sehnert K W and Eisenberg H (1975) *How To Be Your Own Doctor – Sometimes*. New York: Grossett and Dunlap.

Seligman M E P (1975) *Helplessness: On Depression, Development and Death*. San Francisco: W H Freeman.

Sexton D L (1983) Some methodological issues in chronic illness research. *Nursing Research*, **32**(6): 378–380.

Sexton D L and Munro B H (1985) Impact of a husband's chronic illness (COPD) on the spouse's life. *Research in Nursing and Health*, **8**: 83–90.

Shetland M L (1965) Teaching and learning in nursing. *American Journal of Nursing*, **65**(9): 112–116.

Sidaway v Bethlem Royal Hospital Governors and Others (1984) *All England Law Reports*, pp. 1018–1036.

Silva M C and Sorrell J M (1984) Factors influencing comprehension of research. *International Journal of Nursing Studies*, **21**(4): 233–240.

Sitzman J, Kamiya J and Johnson J (1983) Biofeedback training for reduced respiratory rate in chronic obstructive pulmonary disease: a preliminary study. *Nursing Research*, **32**(4): 218–223.

Smith R A, Wallston B S, Wallston K A, Forsberg P R and King J E (1984) Measuring desire for control of health care processes. *Journal of Personality and Social Psychology*, **47**(2): 415–426.

Smith T (1978) Prevention or cure? *British Medical Journal*, **2**: 24.

Speedling E J and Rose D N (1985) Building an effective doctor – patient relationship: from patient satisfaction to patient participation. *Social Science and Medicine*, **21**: 115–120.

Starfield B, Steinwachs D, Morris I, Banse G, Siebert S and Westin C (1979) Patient–doctor agreement about problems needing follow-up visit. *JAMA*, **242**: 344–346.

Starfield B, Wray C, Hess K, Gross R, Birk P S and D'Lugoff B C (1981). Influence of patient – practitioner agreement on outcome of care. *American Journal of Public Health*, **71**: 127–131.

Starr P (1982) *The Social Transformation of American Medicine*. New York: Base Books.

Steele D J, Blackwell B, Gutmann M C and Jackson T C (1987) The activated patient: dogma, dream, or desideratum? *Patient Education and Counseling*, **10**: 3–23.

Stewart N (1988) Commentary. *Lampada*, **14**: 15.

Stilwell B (1986) Evolution, not revolution. *Senior Nurse*, **4**(6): 10–11.

Stimson G V (1974) Obeying doctor's orders: a view from the other side. *Social Science and Medicine*, **8**: 97–104.

Stimson G V and Webb B (1975) *Going to See the Doctor*. London: Routledge and Kegan Paul.

Strickland B R (1965) The prediction of social action from a dimension of internal–external control. *Journal of Social Psychology*, **66**: 353–358.

Strickland B R (1978) Internal–external expectancies and health-related behaviors. *Journal of Consulting and Clinical Psychology*, **46**(6): 1192–1211.

Strull W M, Lo B and Charles G (1984) Do patients want to participate in medical decision making? *JAMA*, **252**(21): 2990–2994.

Suchmann E A (1965) Social patterns of illness and medical care. *Journal of Health and Human Behavior*, **6**: 114–128.

Swenson N (1978) Book review: *Self-Care: Lay Inititatives in Health*. *Social Science and Medicine*, **12A**: 186–188.

Szasz T S and Hollender M H (1956) A contribution to the philosophy of medicine: the basic models of the doctor–patient relationship. *Archives of Internal Medicine*, **97**: 585–592.

Tait K M and Winslow G (1977) Beyond consent – the ethics of decision making in emergency medicine. *Western Medicine*, **126**(2): 156–159.

Thomasma D C (1983) Beyond medical paternalism and patient autonomy: a model of physician conscience for the physician–patient relationship. *Annals of Internal Medicine*, **98**: 243–248.

Timmins N (1988) Warning of £13m legal bill as more patients sue. *The Independent*, 25 March.

Van Dam S, Anderson S and Bauwens E E (1981) *Chronic Health Problems: Concepts and Application.* St Louis: C V Mosby.

Van Den Heuvel W J A (1980) The role of the consumer in health policy. *Social Science and Medicine*, **14A**: 423–426.

Versluyen M (1976) The politics of self-help. *Undercurrents*, **19**: 25, quoted in *Self-Care in Health*, Williamson J D and Danaher K, 1978. London: Croom Helm.

Waitzkin H and Stoeckle J D (1972) The communication of information about illness. *Advances in Psychosomatic Medicine*, **8**: 180–215.

Wallston K A, Wallston B S and DeVillis R (1978) Development of the multidimensional health locus of control (MHLC) scales. *Health Education Monographs*, **6**: 160–171.

Weiss G B (1985) Paternalism modernised. *Journal of Medical Ethics*, **11**: 184–187.

Wilding C, Wells M and Wilson J (1988) A model for family care. *Nursing Times*, **84**(15):38–41.

Williams G (1984) Health promotion – caring concern or slick salesmanship? *Journal of Medical Ethics*, **10**: 191–195.

Williamson J D and Danaher K (1978) *Self-Care in Health*. London: Croom Helm.

Wilson-Barnett J (1978) Patients' emotional responses to barium X-rays. *Journal of Advanced Nursing*, **3**: 37–46.

Wilson-Barnett J (1984) Interventions to alleviate patients' stress: a review. *Journal of Psychosomatic Research*, **28**(1): 63–72.

Wilson-Barnett J (1986) Ethical dilemmas in nursing. *Journal of Medical Ethics*, **12**(3): 12, 123–126, 135.

Wilson-Barnett J and Osborne J (1983) Studies evaluating patient teaching: implications for practice. *International Journal of Nursing Studies*, **20**(1): 33–44.

Winn D (1988) Facing up to fear of the drill. *The Independent*, 12 April.

Wood J and Metcalfe D (1980) Professional attitudes to patient participation groups: an exploratory study. *Journal of the Royal College of General Practitioners*, **30**: 538–541.

Woodward J and Richards D (1977) *Health Care and Popular Medicine in Nineteenth Century England*. London: Croom Helm.

World Health Organisation (1976) Psychosocial factors and health. *WHO Chronicle*, **30**: 337–339.

World Health Organisation (1978) *Alma-Ata 1978: Primary Health Care*. 'Health For All' Series, No. 1. Geneva: WHO.

World Health Organisation (1981) *Global Strategy for Health for All by the Year 2000*. Geneva: WHO.

World Health Organisation, Regional Office for Europe (1984) *Health Promotion: A Discussion Document on the Concept and Principles*. Copenhagen: WHO.

World Health Organisation (1987) *Hospitals and Health For All*. Geneva: WHO.

Wortman C B and Brehm J W (1975) Responses to uncontrollable outcomes: an integration of reactance theory and the learned helplessness model. In *Advances in Experimental Psychology, Vol. 8*, Berkowitz L (ed.). New York: Academic Press.